MARCH TO
A PROMISED LAND

OTHER TITLES IN THE CAPITAL CURRENTS SERIES:

The Ambassador: Inside the Life of a Working Diplomat by John Shaw
Baby at Risk: The Uncertain Legacies of Medical Miracles for Babies, Families, and Society by Ruth Levy Guyer
David, Goliath and the Beach Cleaning Machine: How a Small Polluted Beach Town Fought an Oil Giant—And Won! by Barbara Wolcott
The $100,000 Teacher: A Teacher's Solution to America's Declining Public School System by Brian Crosby
The Other Side of Welfare: A Former Single Welfare Mother Speaks Out by Pamela L. Cave
Torn Between Two Cultures: An Afghan-American Woman Speaks Out by Maryam Qudrat Aseel
Serving Our Children: Charter Schools and the Reform of American Public Education by Kevin Chavous
Suffer the Child: How the Healthcare System Is Failing Our Future by Lidia Wasowicz Pringle

Save 25% when you order any of these and other fine Capital titles from our Web site: www.capital-books.com.

MARCH TO
A PROMISED LAND

The Civil Rights Files of a White Reporter
1952–1968

Al Kuettner

Capital Currents

CAPITAL
BOOKS, INC.
Sterling, Virginia

Capital Books, Inc.
P.O. Box 605
Herndon, Virginia 20172-0605

ISBN 10: 1-933102-28-4 (alk. paper)
ISBN 13: 978-1-933102-28-3

Library of Congress Cataloging-in-Publication Data

Kuettner, Al.
    March to a promised land : the civil rights files of a white reporter, 1952-1968 / Al Kuettner. — 1st ed.
        p. cm. — (Capital currents)
Includes index.
ISBN-13: 978-1-933102-28-3 (alk. paper)
ISBN-10: 1-933102-28-4 (alk. paper)
    1. African Americans—Civil rights—History—20th century. 2. African Americans—Civil rights—Southern States—History—20th century. 3. Civil rights movements—United States—History—20th century. 4. Civil rights movements—Southern States—History—20th century. 5. Kuettner, Al. 6. Journalists—Southern States—Biography. 7. Whites—Southern States—Biography. 8. United States—Race relations—History—20th century. 9. Southern States—Race relations—History—20th century. I. Title. II. Series.

    E185.61.K84 2006
    323.1196'07307809045—dc22

                                                                2006027097

Printed in the United States of America on acid-free paper that meets the American National Standards Institute Z39-48 Standard.

First Edition

10 9 8 7 6 5 4 3 2 1

Dr. Martin Luther King, Jr., speaking in 1963. King's vision for a nonviolent struggle proved effective and focused national attention and support on the Civil Rights Movement. Photo: © Joseph M. Chapman

DEDICATION

This book is dedicated to the UPI reporters and photographers who covered the civil rights story.

In the 1950s and '60s when the Reverend Martin Luther King and other leaders organized protests throughout the segregated South, often at great risk, a legion of news reporters and photographers covered their activities to report to the nation and world what was happening.

These reporters and photographers often braved danger themselves. They have told of threats, beatings, and bullets aimed their way. Notable among these reporters was a phalanx of United Press International employees. UPI had bureaus in every major city and capital of the South, and the agency's stories went around the world. UPI was editorially independent and called them like it saw them, despite threats of retribution. No other news operation covered the story as intensively from the very beginning as UPI did.

CONTENTS

John Lewis (right) and the Reverend Hosea Williams lead marchers over the Pettus Bridge at the start of a march from Selma to Montgomery on March 7, 1965. Moments later state troopers halted the marchers and attacked them with clubs and tear gas. Photo: © Bettmann-Corbis

ACKNOWLEDGMENTS

The editor is a very important element in every news or feature situation. As the writer of this book, I thank my editor, Tobin Beck, whose work was superb. It was during his 2004 visit to my home in Gravette, Arkansas, that the idea of this book came alive. I had started the manuscript 20 years earlier and then set it aside. With Tobin's encouragement and editing, the work was completed.

Hearing and reporting the words of Martin Luther King's "I have a dream" speech from the Lincoln Memorial stands out for me as a particularly strong moment in the Civil Rights story, as does the night I went to King to check out a rumor of his death and heard him say, "Not yet, not yet."

Many of the quotes within this book I heard firsthand from Dr. King and other leaders. Others are drawn from UPI reports and some from additional sources. After all these years I've done my best to cite the sources for material used in this book, looking back to my files and notes that in some cases are more than 50 years old.

We also must recognize and cheer those men of the South who were ready to permit a climate of change in Dixie. It was their baptism into a new and different society.

I particularly thank my wife Helen and son Chris for their love, patience and understanding as I covered this story for so many years.

PREFACE

I am a white Southerner who witnessed and reported about the epic changes that transformed American race relations in the mid- to late-twentieth century. Near the beginning of my career as a reporter for United Press, later United Press International, I traveled extensively throughout the South, talking with hundreds of people, black and white, to get a sense of the frustration, anger, hatred, violence, nonviolent resistance, determination, and hope as those changes evolved. Decades later, as an old man, I retraced my steps, asking black and white whether the changes were worth it. This book is the story of what I found, on both of my journeys.

Let me first tell you a little about myself. I was born in Atlanta, Georgia, into a family that like most others of its generation staunchly believed in racial segregation. The year was 1913, less than fifty years after the Civil War. There were two classes of humanity in my part of the nation; one was the servant class, black people, then called Negroes, the other the master class, called white. The distinction was set, believed to be permanent, and was largely without dispute. This division produced occasional arguments and disputes, at times with violence, but the principal understanding was set: "Nigger" is "Nigger" and "White" is "White." The South and the rest of the nation would go through a major upheaval in correcting that perception.

I encountered prejudice early on. As a young boy in Atlanta, I entered first grade in an all-white neighborhood public school as World War I had ground down to a finish. I don't ever recall hearing a conversation in my family about the war, even though thousands of American troops served and died in that faraway land. It meant nothing to me. School changed that overnight.

My grandparents had emigrated from Germany before the war, and, I suppose, had lived through some tough social times with their German name and foreign accent. That sort of thing was not talked about in range of the children. Nor did my father mention it in my presence. The mention came at school, in the schoolyard, at recess.

"Kaiser," I was branded; stiff-march up and down; hut, hut, hut. Now, these were first-graders, just as I was. Where did they get their intolerance? I spoke "Georgia cracker." There was no television then to deliver the scenario, not even radio. That's the way with prejudice, and still is. Prejudice, the sly "P" word, was introduced to me in this way early in life. That German name, I hated it. I prayed that God would change it. I sank in timid, shamed humiliation each time the roll was called in school and my name came forth in a variety of pronunciations, to the guffaw and hoot of classmates. The cruel fun didn't last long but it remained stuck, like a fishhook, into my memory for years.

After our mother died in the 1918 flu epidemic, my young brother and I became the unofficial wards of two wonderful aunts and an uncle who taught us how to pull bullfrogs out of holes in the creek. I couldn't talk to my father about my miseries, he would just pass off things like that. He was a nice guy in many ways: he once gave me $5 to appease me for having sold my favorite calf.

I recalled that gift sometime later when I overheard a robust argument going on among my elders. A wonderful black lady named *Ola* worked for our family. She would come early to spend the days with my brother and me, stay until after dinner dishes were done, and then walk in all sorts of weather to her streetcar blocks away. That black lady, who was as much family to me as my grownups, had asked that her pay be increased to five dollars a week. Could the raise be afforded? There were three wage earners in the family, but I never knew the answer.

Many years later I recalled the incident when my wife, Helen, decided to give a paid vacation to another black woman who earned considerably more than $5 a week, plus bus fare. That news spread like wildfire in the black community of Atlanta, bringing many a chuckle and causing a brief rebuke from a white and wealthy friend who ended up, after a talk with Helen, doing the same thing.

When I was young the chief means of transportation in Atlanta was the streetcar, used by black and white. The rule was white in front, black in back. Should a white passenger be unable to find a seat up front, the operator yelled out for blacks to move back. Grumbles and subdued anger resulted. Helen as a schoolgirl had skin that bronzed quickly in the summertime. As she boarded one of these crowded cars one morning, the operator caught a glimpse of her as she put her coin in the box. He promptly ordered her to go to the back. With a sly smile she followed the order, much to the grins and winks of the black riders.

By the late 1930s I had learned and absorbed the hometown joys of "Journalism 101" by working at a weekly newspaper in Decatur, just outside

Atlanta. The editor was an old-style Southern gentleman who wore a short beard, had a straight back, and wrote some prize editorials longhand on a school pad.

One day, as I was slaving over an article, the editor yelled, "Come over here, I want to show you something." Another error, I thought. He had spun out of his swivel chair and was standing at the big picture window looking at Sycamore Street. "This, you may not see much longer," he said. It was the local Ku Klux Klan in full regalia, hoods and all, marching through town to a rally. The editor was wrong, wrong, wrong with his belief that the KKK was near collapse. The "bed sheeters," as we boys called them, were still active in places on into the twenty-first century.

It wasn't long before I was offered a job with a worldwide news agency, United Press, known for the integrity of its news coverage. One of my first assignments was to report the annual lynching statistics researched by Tuskegee Institute, a then-struggling black college in Alabama. That was my baptism into what was called the "segregation story."

By the 1940s the segregation issue had heated up, focusing on what was called separate but equal public school education for black pupils. In 1952 the U.S. Supreme Court agreed to listen to the subject. In preparation, the court invited to Washington spokesmen on both sides of the issue, a novel approach to information gathering that for a spell laid aside the law books and listened to voices. Off and on for two years the court listened, asking questions. I remained glued to the developing issue—reporting the fallout. In 1954 the court handed down its decision: in public education, racial discrimination is unconstitutional.

The next morning Stanley Whitaker, the division manager of United Press in the South, called me into a meeting. He predicted that this would be both an instant and long-range social issue in the South and in the nation. He added that the population knew very little of the consequences. "We want you to get in your car and make a tour of the South," he said. "Find out what the people think. When can you leave?" It was a short meeting. I left Atlanta the next day.

Thus began a twenty-year journey that took me to report on the work, and later murder, of Dr. Martin Luther King Jr., and that took me to a meeting on the front porch of a plantation home on the Mississippi Delta. It was there that I visited with a wrinkled old black farmer. He had not heard of the court decision. He repeatedly and softly chanted "thank God" as the development was explained to him. "But where are the children?" I asked him. "I have come a long way and I see no children on the Delta. Where are the children?"

He replied, somewhat sadly, somewhat proudly: "They gone north. They getting educated. But soon as they can, they be back; they be coming home." It was a prediction that came true.

One of the searing, permanent memories of my thousand-mile reporter's journey is of a good white fellow, in the midst of a little racial demonstration, in a little street, in a little town in what was called the "Deep South." For a few seconds we stood eyeball-to-eyeball, close enough for his tortured spit to spray my face, which it did. "You son of a bitch," he screamed. "Why don't you go home and let us handle this!" The year was 1953.

The anguish would get worse. Oh, yes, there was to be Birmingham, Little Rock, Jackson, St. Augustine, and a once-quiet little postcard-like town called Selma. I learned to live with their lamentations, but I never forgot the pitiful cry of that one good native white Southerner whose name I never knew. It's been more than a half-century since that special day, but I still remember how he, for a few dramatic moments, held center stage and sang the requiem of the Old South.

I visualize him even now as a hard-working son of the soil; his hands and face are like old wood. He's good to his black help. Wasn't he the one they were writing about who paid all the hospital bills for the dark family whose mother was dying? Didn't the grieving family ask him to pray at the funeral? I know one thing for certain; that poor man would do all sorts of good in his life, but there is one thing he would not do: He would not cross the color line.

After all these years, and after all the progress toward racial tolerance in America, I had about decided to let the subject rest from further dissertation. The racial darkness of the twentieth century had blended into the advancing sunlight of the twenty-first. African-Americans (as they were by then acknowledged) could walk into any public eating place in the fifty states, enroll at any public education institution, and check into any resting place open to the public. Then, one day, a young high school student, at the close of a class where I had guest-lectured, said to me, "We have it in history books but I still don't understand it; please tell me the story of what happened."

Shall we start from the beginning?

MARCH TO
A PROMISED LAND

Attorneys who argued the case against segregation stand together smiling in front of the U.S. Supreme Court in Washington, D.C., after the court ruled that segregation in public schools is unconstitutional. Left to right are George E.C. Hayes of Washington, D.C.; Thurgood Marshall, special counsel for the NAACP; and James Nabrit, Jr., professor and attorney at Howard University in Washington. Photo: © Bettmann-Corbis

CHAPTER 1

1954–Supreme Court Bans
Segregated Schools

"Give me some pride."   —Black Student

*"If men could learn from history, what lessons it might teach us!
But passion and party blind our eyes . . ."*

—Samuel Taylor Coleridge

One day in 1952 I inserted a fresh file folder into the drawer of my desk at the old United Press bureau in Atlanta, Georgia, and casually labeled it "Segregation."

How wrong I was to think that this was a casual subject, for soon it would fill many file folders in my desk. For two decades in the mid-twentieth century, racial segregation was probably the most written-about, talked-about, hailed and damned topic of the time. It provoked assassination and brought about the downfall of some governments and radical changes in others. It competed for attention with wars and monarchs and presidents.

I became deeply involved in sifting out this story for a populace unprepared and without rules or emotional balance to deal with it. Few recognized in the year 1952 where this story of segregation would go; fewer realized that its outreach would change the course of history in the United States and the world in a very short time.

The strongest stirrings at first were in the South, for it was here that most blacks in the United States lived. It was a confusing time, and not just for whites. I was surprised at the number of relatively secure—as well as fearful—blacks who shrank from thoughts of change.

In the South—but also in some other areas that boasted openly of non-discrimination—segregation was a way of life. It meant simply the separation of the black and white races by custom, practice, tradition, or law. One or all of these applications of the word extended to schools, churches, living places, public libraries, hospitals, public conveyances, public drinking fountains, swimming pools, seaside bathing beaches, public eating places—everything.

Blacks had tried for many years to break the bonds of segregation, never losing the dream of a chance to leave their physical and mental ghetto, if they desired. Slaves killed themselves to escape being owned; rioted, killed, were strung up on tree limbs. A writer in *Essays in the History of the American Negro* observed that they never let the world forget their oppression and enslavement.

"They purchased their freedom where possible, they . . . cut off their fingers and hands, they refused to work, and were tortured. They fled to swamps, and congregated, and waged war. They fled to havens of liberty— to invading armies, to the Indians, to the Canadians, to the Dutch, to the French, to the Spaniards and Mexicans, and to the Northern states.

"They went from door to door seeking money wherewith to purchase the freedom of their parents, wives, or children. They went from city to city explaining, pleading, warning, agitating. They wrote pamphlets, letters and books telling of the plight of their people and urging reform or rebellion. They plotted or rebelled, alone or with the poor whites, time and time again, and the corpses of the martyrs were barely cold before others sprang forward to give their lives' blood to the struggle."

Their children and their children's children tried other methods, but always the result was incomplete—until the mid-twentieth century.

There were those in that period who believed that the only way to repair the cultural damage was through the drastic step of eliminating separate education systems for black and white. The heart of the matter was school segregation in the seventeen states and the nation's capital where black and white youngsters were prevented by law from attending the same public schools.

In 1952 the Supreme Court of the United States announced that it would begin hearings on a case that had come before it for review: *Brown v. Board of Education*. It was a case to test the constitutionality of segregated public education. There was ample evidence that, whatever the Founding Fathers and the Congress had meant by freedom from segregation, the mandates had not been followed in the practice of supplying education. But was the practice constitutional? That is what the court had to decide.

The Declaration of Independence in America said on July 4, 1776: "We hold these truths to be self-evident, that all men are created equal, that they are endowed by their Creator with certain unalienable rights, that among these are Life, Liberty and the pursuit of Happiness. . . . That whenever any form of government becomes destructive of these ends, it is the right of the people to alter or to abolish it, and to institute new government. . . ."

The Fourteenth Amendment to the Constitution of the United States said it another way on June 13, 1866, one year after the end of the Civil War: "No state shall make or enforce any law which shall abridge the privileges or immunities of citizens of the United States; nor shall any state deprive any person of Life, Liberty, or Property, without due process of law; nor deny to any person within its jurisdiction the equal protection of the laws."

The document was proclaimed "the Supreme Law of the Land" . . . "and the judges in every state shall be bound thereby, anything in the Constitution or laws of any State to the contrary notwithstanding."

It was proposed by Congress on February 26, 1869, that a Fifteenth Amendment be added to the Constitution. Submitted to the states and approved by the required two-thirds majority, it was declared ratified March 30, 1870. It stated: "The right of citizens of the United States to vote shall not be denied or abridged by the United States or by any State on account of race, color, or previous condition of servitude. The Congress shall have power to enforce this article by appropriate legislation."

All of these pronouncements, whether or not they concerned education directly, had a part in what the high court was now considering, as did a case that had been decided in 1896. That year, the Supreme Court had approved the doctrine that state laws requiring separate accommodations did not offend against the Constitution's equal protection clause if the separated facilities were "substantially equal." The ruling came in the case of Plessy v. Ferguson, a case out of Louisiana. Louisiana law of 1890 required all railway companies to provide separate accommodations for blacks and whites. Homer Plessy, believed to be seven-eighths white, refused to vacate a seat in a white compartment and was arrested.

In the post-Civil War years stretching toward 1952 there were numerous court decisions, and acts of Congress affirmed and re-affirmed the basic tenets of the American system of government. Yet, these freedoms still were not fully realized, or recognized. Thousands of black Americans were deprived of full citizenship rights.

Despite the upheavals and some improvements in their lot in the past, the sting of discrimination against black people remained. In many parts of

America, blacks could not vote, they were forbidden to eat or live in certain areas, public accommodations for them were restricted, and their public school education was segregated and often inferior.

From mediocre schools, black children came home to relatives who in another generation had gone to even more inferior schools, if, indeed, they had gone to school at all. And so the cycle was repeated. (It should be noted that there were cases of black children attending white public schools in parts of the South. This had been going on for many years, but it barely merits mention, for it was certainly not a pattern. Most often, such cases were matters of convenience in a local school district, and tightly controlled.)

Wealthy individuals and agencies outside the South financed some of the best education for Southern black pupils through establishment of private schools and contributions to libraries, scholarships, and other cultural outlets. But only a very small proportion of the brightest black children were affected. For the greatest majority of the black population, one generation of inferiority passed it on to the next.

That was the situation in 1952 when the Supreme Court agreed to get into the argument once again. The best strategic location from which to watch the fallout developments of this episode in the nation's history was the South. A journalist in that region could often commute—or walk—to the story. That's what I sometimes did, finding it within easy reach of the news bureau in Atlanta.

The case chosen for review by the Supreme Court was not a Southern case at all. The Reverend Oliver Brown, a Topeka, Kansas, clergyman, brought the suit on behalf of his fifteen-year-old daughter, Linda. He claimed that she had to travel twenty blocks to a black school, although a white school was only four blocks from her home.

The case of Linda Brown became famous as the keystone of legal action to topple public school segregation; yet, here was a case that did not need to happen. Nelson R. Ober of the *Topeka Daily Capital*, reporting for the *Southern School News*, found that Topeka was actually out-distancing the court developments and taking steps to integrate all school facilities before Linda Brown ever reached high school. Her father and others had filed their desegregation suit against the Topeka Board of Education when his daughter was in the third grade of then-segregated Monroe Elementary School. The arguments on which the high court reached its decision reflected conditions before Topeka integrated all of its schools.

Kansas, its black population sparse, appeared to be an unusual place to test a constitutional issue on race. The state had no law or constitutional restrictions that required school segregation, although Kansas did have a law permitting segregation in the high schools of Kansas City, Kansas, and in the elementary schools of the twelve cities in the state with more than fifteen thousand population. One of those twelve was Topeka, which had eighteen elementary schools for whites and four for blacks, and where blacks were admitted to the city swimming pool one day out of the year. That was in the era before change set in voluntarily in Topeka.

On Tuesday, December 9, 1952, Robert L. Carter, graduate of Lincoln University, the University of Pennsylvania, the Howard University Law School and Columbia University, stood before the Supreme Court and stated the case for his client, Linda Brown.

"Negro children in Topeka, Kansas," said the black attorney for the National Association for the Advancement of Colored People, ". . . were placed at a serious disadvantage with their opportunity to develop citizenship skills, and were denied the opportunity to learn to adjust personally and socially in a setting comprising a cross-section of the dominant population of the city."

Throughout the long court arguments, I found no evidence or questions pertaining to the fact that Topeka already was removing its segregation rules. The chief justice of the United States, Fred M. Vinson, of Kentucky, was presiding. The nine-member court ranged from conservative, to moderate, to liberal in its philosophy.

Carter informed the court that in Topeka, "Negro children are put in one category for public school purposes, solely on the basis of race and color, and white children are put in another category for the purpose of determining what schools they will attend."

Justice Minton: "Mr. Carter, I don't know whether I have followed you or all the facts on this. Was there a finding (in lower courts) that the only basis of classification was race or color?"

Carter: "It was admitted . . . that the only reason that they would not permit Negro children to attend the 18 white schools was because they were Negro."

Justice Reed: "Was there any evidence in the record to show the inability, the lesser ability of the child in the segregated schools?"

Carter: "Yes, sir, there was a great deal of testimony on the impact of racial distinctions and segregation on the emotional and mental development of the child . . ."

The court had been besieged and bedeviled by every side of this issue in its effort to find the truth. The court had all the books on the subject and almost more than was wanted of "expert" advice. Now the justices were eager to find the evidence. "The evidence, Mr. Carter, what was the evidence?"

Carter: "The evidence, yes, sir. The evidence went to the fact that in the segregated school, because of the emotional impact that segregation has, it does impair the ability to learn . . . and that, further, you are barred from contact with members of the dominant group and, therefore, your total education content is somewhat lower than it would be ordinarily."

The Supreme Court hearings lasted off and on for almost two years. Similar suits from South Carolina, Delaware, and Virginia were added to *Brown v. Board of Education*. The case was given "class" status, meaning that a decision would apply to everyone with situations similar to those few who had sued.

The South Carolina case concerned Clarendon County, forty miles southeast of Columbia, the state capital. Clarendon, bordered by the Santee River, is the site of a huge national wildlife preserve, and Francis Marion, the famous "Swamp Fox" of Revolutionary times, is buried on a site overlooking the river. At the time of the court case, Clarendon had a population of thirty-two thousand, seven out of ten black.

Levi Pearson, black father of three school children, agreed to file a federal court suit asking that school bus transportation be provided in Clarendon County for black children. That's all he wanted. His case was filed in 1948 in a lower federal court, and he lost it on a technicality. The Reverend J. A. Delaine dusted off the failed effort, and it was his case that landed in the Supreme Court.

The Delaware case had its origin in 1951 in a state court hearing before the chancellor of Delaware, Collins Seitz. During the hearing, Frederic Wertham, chief resident psychiatrist at Johns Hopkins Hospital in Baltimore, later a member of the medical faculty at New York University that operated Bellevue Hospital in New York, was a leading testifier. Wertham became a noted psychiatrist with special interest in blacks.

"It isn't enough to look at the child and say, 'This little girl doesn't have nightmares; she gets by in school; she doesn't annoy anyone at home; she isn't a juvenile delinquent'—that is not enough," Wertham told the court. "I hold the scientific opinion that if a rosebush should produce twelve roses, and if only one rose grows, it is not a healthy rosebush. It is up to us to find out what is interfering with its growth and with its health."

Wertham argued that segregation in public and high school creates in the mind of the child "an unsolvable conflict, an unsolvable emotional conflict, and I would say an inevitable conflict." He said that because white and black schools were "vastly different" in Claymont, Delaware, "most of the children we have examined interpret segregation in one way, and only one way—and that is they interpret it as punishment."

During the earlier state court hearing, Chancellor Seitz personally went to observe conditions of black and white schools. He expressed himself as being "appalled" at conditions in the black schools. He ruled that eleven black children in Claymont were entitled to immediate admission to white schools. It was the first time a segregated white public school in the United States was ordered by a court to admit black children. His 1951 decision was appealed and carried to the Supreme Court.

Prince Edward County, Virginia, dates its origin to 1753, when its 356-square-mile area was given the name of the grandnephew of England's King George III. The population was approximately half black and half white when its desegregation case went to the Supreme Court on behalf of a sixteen-year-old black girl, Barbara Johns.

On a reporting trip to Farmville in Prince Edward County, I visited the new black high school, built and equipped with no expense spared in an effort to ensure equal, though separate, school facilities. By comparison, Farmville High School for white pupils was old and drab.

There in Farmville, I met an extraordinary porch-swing philosopher, an elderly black man of indefinite age. He was swaying slowly, his eyes half closed, as I approached. We talked for an hour as he unraveled a tale of hard work in an effort to educate his children.

"My daughter, she wanted to teach," he said with a touch of sadness, "but there was no place here for her to learn. She had to go away. Now she is a teacher but she can't come home because they don't take teachers like her except in the Negro schools."

He was interrupted by the ringing of a school bell. Across the way at the State Teachers College the grounds were suddenly filled with students on class break. All of them were white. "That's what I mean," he said.

I told him I had just visited the new high school for black students. "Why would they want to go to the white school that is not as good as their own?" I asked. His answer came with fire in an old voice: "You white people won't understand that it's not just a nice building that counts."

The hearings before the Supreme Court attracted the most thunderous barrage of oratory since Henry Clay (like Chief Justice Vinson, also of Kentucky) stood before the U.S. Senate in 1830 and proclaimed: "Mr. President, I am no friend of slavery . . . but I prefer the liberty of my own country to that of any other people, the liberty of my own race to that of any other race."

On one side of this newer case were the best White Supremacy lawyers to be found—a formidable array that would have shaken a less confident and prepared opponent. But this time the opponent was prepared; indeed, this case had been in preparation not for a few weeks, but for years. Its help came from those who never sought nor held the spotlight.

Austin T. Walden of Atlanta, an elder statesman among black lawyers, did not stand in the court to argue, but he wrote significant portions of the argument to end segregation in the schools. He had put in his share of legal time helping blacks out of Saturday night lockups, but he had spent more time counseling bright young black students, urging them to learn the law if they really wanted to bring an end to racial segregation.

President Johnson, in a message at the time of Walden's death, paid him high tribute, saying that for many years Austin Walden was the only friend of blacks in trouble. It was an appropriate accolade. In 1912, just out of law school, Walden tried his first murder case, defending a black man who had killed another black in self-defense. The man on trial claimed the other had advanced on him, hand in a pocket, and he had shot him when the assailant was twenty feet away. Walden talked with witnesses, twelve of whom said it was self-defense. But the white employer of the dead man was said to have intimidated the witnesses, and they changed their stories on the witness stand. The defendant was sentenced to hang.

Walden was crushed, but a few weeks after the trial he was visited by the white sheriff and another county official. They told him they were suspicious of the trial results because it was the first time a black had been sentenced in the county to hang for killing another black. They told Walden they had checked and found there were three reasons the defendant had been found guilty: Walden was a "nigger lawyer"; he acted as though he were at home in the courtroom; and he drank out of the glass with everybody else. They decided, by God, they would just hang his client. The officers promised to help Walden gain a new trial for his client, and there he won an acquittal.

Relating the story to me years later, Walden chuckled over the memory and said the experience helped mold his philosophy throughout his legal career. He realized that a half-century before, there were white men in the Deep South who had the character to stand for principle, regardless of race. Walden was respected and admired in courtrooms of the South many years before the civil rights developments of the mid-twentieth century.

The "Colonel," as he was called before he became the first black judge in Atlanta, was never racist although he fought as long and hard as any on the civil rights trail to bring dignity and opportunity to blacks. As lawyer and citizen, he quietly influenced many a change in racial understanding. He and his family lived in a comfortable but unpretentious home in Atlanta, and I had the feeling that his lifestyle was due in part to his modest resources.

I suspect that throughout his career he dispensed more free legal advice than what he was paid for.

Walden's modesty extended to his every activity. Often he entered a courtroom without notice, responding silently to a judge who acknowledged his presence with a nod. Sometimes he was at the defense table, at others with the prosecution. In his later years he rarely argued cases, but his advice was strong and effective.

I see him now, sitting there in silence. Presently, his eyes close and he appears to have nodded off. Opposing lawyers learned to disregard that habit, for the Colonel was not sleeping. He leans forward and whispers to an attorney; more than once what he said would be the key to the case. It was not unusual for a judge to call Walden to the bench to straighten out some fine legal point. Once during a federal court hearing, the case was recessed while the Colonel went to his modest office to research a needed fact in his library.

Walden's philosophy was that good law was meant to serve all the people, with no discrimination because of race, religion, or station in life. And he argued constantly for bad law to be repealed. Because he believed in the law and in justice, he was highly regarded, even by the young activists of the civil rights movement who criticized him for being "so slow." And when it came time to be an activist, everyone knew where he stood.

I was waiting by the sixth-floor elevator door in Atlanta's Rich's Department Store the day that the tearoom was integrated. For weeks the beloved old Magnolia Room had been closed, its chairs stacked and tables bare, while young blacks campaigned to break the segregation barrier there. Atlanta whites who had come there for years were subjected to standing in corners to munch sandwiches while black and white negotiators argued over an agreement. Finally, Rich's gave in and the historic time was set for change. Walden, again because of a respect that crossed racial lines, was chosen to lead the first small group of blacks into the Magnolia Room. He emerged quietly from the elevator and with great dignity walked into the tea room, its tables now back in perfect order. In such ways, he helped his changing Southland over its hurdles.

Many black students responded to appeals from Walden and others, and a number gravitated to the Howard University Law School in Washington, D.C., a small school in those days but with a distinguished faculty. There, students like Thurgood Marshall, who was to argue for the plaintiffs in *Brown v. Board of Education*, and later would sit on the U.S. Supreme Court, learned the law. They mastered the technique of finding evidence; more importantly, they learned how not to get sidetracked or derailed by a smart lawyer on the other side. These young black attorneys carefully built the mountain of evidence that finally came in 1952 to the nine justices of the Supreme Court.

Lawyers on both sides of the issue submitted volumes of written words, and spoke volumes more. The court listened, prodded both sides, and contemplated what its members knew would be a landmark decision. During the period of the hearings, Chief Justice Vinson, an appointee of President Truman, a Democrat, died in 1953, and was succeeded by Earl Warren of California, appointed by President Eisenhower, a Republican.

The hearings narrowed to a tough legal battle between Thurgood Marshall for desegregation and John W. Davis of South Carolina, then 79, a former Democratic presidential candidate, for the side of segregation.

Marshall and Spottswood W. Robinson teamed up to argue the case for desegregation of schools in Prince Edward County, Virginia. Opposing them were the colorful Davis and Justin Moore. Robinson came quickly to the point: that black children were being denied their rights secured by the Fourteenth Amendment.

"Our position is this," said Robinson, ". . . that the (Fourteenth) amendment had as its purpose and effect the complete legal equality of all persons, irrespective of race, and the prohibition of all state-imposed caste and class systems based upon race; and . . . that segregation in public schools . . . is necessarily embraced within the prohibition of the Amendment."

Robinson then reviewed congressional action that led to the Fourteenth Amendment, noting that when the Thirty-Ninth Congress, which formulated the amendment, convened in December 1865, it was confronted with so-called "Black Codes" in the South. Under these codes, laws were designed to maintain the inferior position of blacks that existed prior to abolition of slavery. They resulted in blacks having to work for limited pay, restricted their mobility, prohibited testimony in court against a white person, contained innumerable provisions for segregation on carriers and in public places and, in some cases, "expressed prohibitions upon the attendance by Negroes of the public schools provided for white children."

The issue of states' rights was introduced by Justice Frankfurter. "I suggest that the question is not whether this court loses its power, but whether the states lose their power."

Thurgood Marshall had a ready answer: "As of this time, we have a test to see whether or not the public policy, customs and mores of the states of South Carolina and Virginia, or the avowed intent of our Constitution—as to which one will prevail."

Easily one of the most persuasive lawyers on the side of continued segregation was Davis of South Carolina—veteran of half a century's courtroom battles. He reminded the justices that South Carolina had promised a previous court that the state would remove inequalities as soon as possible, and indeed had moved in that direction.

"We have then (in South Carolina) a case . . . with no remaining question of inequality at all, and the naked question is whether a separation of the races in the primary and secondary schools . . . is of itself per se a violation of the 14th Amendment," Davis argued.

". . . The overwhelming preponderance of the evidence demonstrates that the Congress which submitted, and the state legislatures which ratified, the 14th Amendment did not understand that it would abolish segregation in public schools."

Referring to Clarendon, South Carolina School District Number 1, one of the cases being argued, Davis said:

"There were in the last report that got into this record . . . 2,799 registered Negro children of school age. There were 295 whites, and the state has now provided those 2,800 Negro children with schools as good in every particular. In fact, because of their being newer, they may be even better. There are good teachers and the same curriculum as in the schools for the 295 whites."

"Who is going to disturb that situation? If they were to be re-assorted or co-mingled, who knows how that could best be done? If it is done on the mathematical basis, with 30 children as a maximum, which I believe is the accepted standard in pedagogy, you would have 27 Negro children and three whites in one schoolroom. Would that make the children any happier? Would they learn any more quickly? Would their lives be more serene?

"Children of that age are not the most considerate animals in the world, as we all know. Would the terrible psychological disaster being wrought— according to some of these witnesses—to the colored child be removed if he had three white children sitting somewhere in the same school room? Would white children be prevented from getting a distorted idea of race relations if they sat with 27 Negro children?"

Davis argued that South Carolina was not before the court in "sackcloth and ashes," but rather was moving in good faith to produce equality for all of its children of whatever race or color.

"It is convinced that the happiness, the progress, and the welfare of these children is best promoted in segregated schools, and it thinks it a thousand pities that by this controversy there should be urged the return to an experiment which gives no more promise of success today than when it was written into their Constitution during what I call the tragic era," Davis said.

"I am reminded . . . of Aesop's fable of the dog and the meat. The dog, with a fine piece of meat in his mouth, crossed a bridge and saw his reflection in the stream, and plunged for it, and lost both substance and shadow. Here is equal education, not promised, not prophesied, but present. Shall it be thrown away on some fancied question of racial prestige?"

Spottswood W. Robinson III returned to the Virginia case, focusing on the Prince Edward County town of Farmville, thirty miles east of Appomattox where the Civil War ended.

"Farmville High School, one of the two white high schools, is a school which is accredited by the Southern Association of Colleges and Secondary Schools, while the Moton School for Negroes is not," Robinson explained to the court. "As a consequence of this accreditation, the white graduate of Farmville will generally be admitted to institutions of higher learning outside the state on his record alone, while Negro graduates of Moton will generally be required to take examinations to get in, or, if admitted without examination, will be accorded only a probationary status."

So these were the cases before the Supreme Court:

- Topeka, Kansas–A child who walked twenty blocks to a black school, past a white school four blocks from her home.
- Clarendon County, South Carolina–A black father asking for school bus transportation for black children.
- Claymont, Delaware–An effort to end the "emotional conflict" in segregated black children.
- Prince Edward County, Virginia–A case based on denial of Fourteenth Amendment rights of black children.

Following the hearings, the Supreme Court justices went their individual ways to study, to research, to write. For months the public had no inkling of what the court would do with *Brown v. Board of Education*. Then came May 17, 1954. It was the ninety-first year since the Emancipation Proclamation and the fifty-eighth year since another Supreme Court ruled that education facilities could be separate so long as they were equal.

There was no advance word that the court would hold more than a routine session on May 17. For the first forty minutes, new lawyers were admitted to practice before the court, bringing former Secretary of State Dean Acheson to present his son. Experienced observers noted, however, that as the justices filed in, a recently empty chair was occupied. Justice Robert H. Jackson, absent for several weeks because of a heart attack, took his place to complete the nine-member panel. Attorney General Herbert Brownell sat at the government desk in only his third appearance in the courtroom since his appointment 16 months before. In the celebrities' section there were some visitors who rarely came to court, including Mrs. Earl Warren, wife of the chief justice, and Mrs. Herbert Brownell, wife of the attorney general.

After all the preliminaries were disposed of, the chief justice said quietly: "I have the court's opinion and decision in No. 1, 2, 4, and 10, *Oliver Brown v. Board of Education.*"

In the courtroom, United Press reporter Ruth Gmeiner took notes and sent them by pneumatic tube to the UP office in the Supreme Court press-room, where UP reporter Charlotte Moulton read them but waited to file until she heard from Gmeiner what the court had decided.

". . . Therefore," Chief Justice Warren read, "we hold that the plaintiffs and others similarly situated, for whom the actions have been brought are, by reason of the segregation complained of, deprived of the equal protection of the laws guaranteed by the Fourteenth Amendment . . ."

At one minute after noon, in the midst of an item on routine happenings in Washington, a teletype machine in the Atlanta newsroom of United Press suddenly stopped as though to catch its breath, and then erupted with a clanging of bells—signal that a matter of great importance was about to be transmitted.

As the account from Room 31 in the nation's Supreme Court began moving by teletype into newsrooms around the nation and the world, I reached for a telephone on my desk in Atlanta and dialed the office of Georgia Attorney General Eugene Cook. For years he had fought untiringly to preserve Georgia's stand on racial segregation. "Separate but equal" was his credo and his personal conviction. Gene Cook really wanted education to be equal but, equal or not, he wanted it to remain separate.

"Gene, the decision just came in," I told him. "'The U.S. Supreme Court ruled today that racial segregation in the public schools is unconstitutional.'"

It was ten minutes past noon.

Looking back, I am certain that Cook required only a few seconds to reply, but it seemed like hours before he spoke. "I'm sorry," he responded wearily. "It means we are headed for a whole generation of litigation."

His words were prophetic.

One consequence of the Supreme Court decision was hateful fear. I have seen otherwise decent people salivate with it, mouths twitching and frothing.

This was the dross dredged up from the great melting pot of America by the decision of the highest court in the land.

Another consequence of the *Brown* case, and of more significance—although slower to develop—was understanding. People were forced to inquire into their own motives, prejudices, and fears that had been brought into focus by the high court's stand that racial segregation was unconstitutional.

In the years following the momentous decision, one effort after another was made in the South to avoid a complete collapse of the old system in which there had been a fragile understanding between white and black.

There was segregation, token integration, separate but equal facilities that often gave black children far better schools than white; and there was negotiation in which each side took a little and gave a little.

Doctrines, policies, legislation, and firebrand oratory were used to define the relationship between two races of Americans. There would be many obstacles to overcome before the 1954 school decision was fully implemented.

A paratrooper from the 101ˢᵗ Airborne Division stands guard outside Central High School in Little Rock, Arkansas, on September 25, 1957, as students chat during a fire drill. The troops integrated Central, ending a month of open defiance of federal authority. The nine black students were taken to the school in an Army vehicle guarded by two jeeploads of soldiers. Photo: © Bettmann-Corbis

CHAPTER 2

1957–Integration Dixie Style: Little Rock

"There must be a beginning of any great matter, but the continuing unto the end until it be thoroughly finished yields the true glory."

—Sir Francis Drake

Now came the time for testing, and it went on for years. The material in my file drawer increased rapidly. The impact of the May 17, 1954, school desegregation decision was soon felt at the school district level, now that there was a clear mandate with the force of law which wiped out a nineteenth-century "separate but equal" doctrine of an earlier court.

"Nigger, go home!"

Opening of the 1954 fall school term in the South produced a mixed pattern: compliance, wait-and-see, outright defiance. Four states were in the defying category: Georgia, Louisiana, Mississippi, and South Carolina. Nine others among the seventeen states with required public school segregation adopted a stance of "awaiting court action." They were Alabama, Arkansas, Florida, Kentucky, North Carolina, Oklahoma, Tennessee, Texas, and Virginia. Delaware, Maryland, Missouri, West Virginia, and the District of Columbia took steps—some slowly, others rapidly—to comply with the court decision. Four other states with permissive segregation (Arizona, Kansas, New Mexico, and Wyoming) announced they were complying with the decision.

In North Carolina, Asheville and Charlotte began "compliance studies." Oklahoma opened college and university enrollments to both races, and local districts were asked by the State Education Department to begin desegregation at once. South Carolina, through a Special Segregation Study Committee,

19

recommended that schools remain separate, and in that state, Clarendon County (one of the parties in the 1954 Supreme Court case) announced it would close schools before permitting integration. Tennessee announced gradual desegregation for the six state-supported colleges. Virginia said it would remain segregated, and its Prince Edward County (another party in the 1954 case) began raising $212,000 to assure white teachers of their jobs if public schools were closed. Florida adopted a pupil assignment act giving counties the right to continue segregation. The Georgia legislature studied ways to circumvent integration. The Kentucky Board of Education urged local districts to begin integration "as rapidly as possible." Louisiana and Mississippi stood firm in their determination to remain segregated. And four of the five largest school districts in Arkansas revealed desegregation plans.

Although moving cautiously on elementary and secondary school desegregation, Arkansas dated its admission of black university students back to February 1948 when Silas Hunt, twenty-three, a World War II combat veteran, enrolled at the University of Arkansas Law School in Fayetteville. At the same time, Wiley Branton, who later became the leading civil rights lawyer in Arkansas, attempted to enroll in the University of Arkansas College of Business Administration but was turned down. Two years later, he was admitted to the University of Arkansas Law School from which he graduated in 1952. He and Thurgood Marshall were the petitioners in 1958 for desegregation of Little Rock, Arkansas, public schools.

It was quite a game that school districts, cities, counties, and states played in those days, spending weeks in courts over alleged constitutional rights that already had been declared unconstitutional.

And what of the children? What effect did this adult-generated confusion have on their psyche, their ability to learn? In the short range, the effect was destructive but not disastrous. Hearing screaming crowds outside the building was not the best atmosphere for learning, but studies bear out the fact that the harm was not long-lasting. Those who were motivated to teach and learn taught and learned, regardless of the confusion. What interested me were the simple ways in which young children resolved their black and white feelings and differences.

In Atlanta, Georgia, during the first experiences at a desegregated elementary school, a fight erupted between two boys, one black and the other white. When the white teacher separated the combatants and calmed their fury, she asked what the problem was. "He said I had springy hair," the black child blurted. "Well, you do have springy hair, and it is very pretty," the teacher said. Then she asked the white child if he had ever touched springy hair and the eager response was no but he would like to. With the black boy's permission, the white child placed a hand gently on the other's head. Smiles broke on both their faces, and they walked away as friends in a new environment.

So it was with skin. Skin was a barrier to understanding and communications as much as anything else. I've heard it said quite seriously, "Don't touch black skin. It will come off on you." All of us notice differences. Have you had the experience of living in an area where there were no black people, or no white people, and have you seen one of the other color at the theater or the grocer's? Your attention is suddenly, and even unconsciously, riveted on the one uncommon to your experience.

A wise teacher I knew in Atlanta during those experimental first days of integrated classes tried very hard to win the confidence of her black pupils. One day at the lunch hour a black child, sitting at her side, shyly touched the teacher's arm and began rubbing. In wonder, she looked up at the white woman and said softly, "Your skin feels just like ours."

The books and television playbacks about that period are filled with the passions of school desegregation, but not enough is remembered about how individuals dealt with the transition in little ways that built bridges of understanding, fragile though they were at first. It was hardest on the white grownups—worried about the jobs they feared "the niggers" would take, fearful their white daughters would be raped by blacks, fearful their children could not learn if blacks were in the same school, fearful their neighborhoods would be destroyed. I know of white children who were severely punished at home for speaking to a black pupil at school in the early days of desegregation. This may have caused some of the aggressive behavior at school—showing Dad that "I hate niggers."

Under these conditions, with what commitment would the U.S. government require that the high court decision be enforced?

You had to walk in the footsteps of these people—black and white—to get some understanding of their deep feelings, their prejudices; the sad deprivation suffered by so many blacks, the fear in whites. You had to walk and talk with them, and that's what I did for fifteen years, knowing that this story could not unfold from reading propaganda statements from both sides of the controversy. This was a people story.

I came upon a touching situation in Greenville, Mississippi, where a private Roman Catholic school was helping black adult women reach an education level that would qualify them for jobs. The school made use of hand-cut individual letters, often brightly colored and with rough edges, developed by Maria Montessori, physician and educator, in the slums of Italy. With this device, illiterates got the feel of letters of the alphabet by rubbing fingers over the rough surface.

A woman had come for weeks to the Greenville school, laboriously learning to read and write. Her time of triumph finally came, and, with tears running down her face, she told her teacher: "My little girl has been reading to me because I couldn't read. Last night I read to her for the first time."

During those years of racial adjustment and transition I spent a lot of time talking with teachers. One was a white woman in Atlanta. She was born and spent her early life in a small Georgia town where blacks outnumbered whites, and where her parents, her grandparents, and all of her family were ardent segregationists.

In the changing situation after Atlanta was ordered to desegregate public schools, she asked to be transferred from her comfortable, middle-class white school to an inner-city school that was suddenly predominantly black. She was no crusader, nor a bleeding heart liberal. "I was just thrilled with the chance to find out if I could teach there," she told me. She said she was surprised to discover how simple it was.

"When they [the school authorities] started talking about the school, I said, 'Let me take it. It's the first school I've been in where they take the child exactly where he is.' There will be children in the seventh grade being taught in second-grade books. Usually, the school staff said, 'All right, you're in the third grade, everybody's going to work in the third-grade books.' I like the idea that in the new school, the real secret is going to be the teachers."

She quickly found there was a large gap between what her black pupils heard, what they saw, and what they said. They had hearing difficulties that made it hard for them to distinguish between long and short vowels. "Their ears are just tuned out, so I'm starting with them from the standpoint of what they see. Gradually, they stop saying 'dis' and 'dat,' 'dem' and 'hit.' Broad 'a' begins to disappear."

One of the brightest children in her third-grade class was a black child who didn't know where the third grade was, or that he was in the wrong place. It was three days before the school discovered he was in the fourth grade by mistake. "He didn't do well at first. Now, I have already moved him up from one reading group to another because he catches on so quickly, and he's beginning to hear phonics. Suddenly, he will say: 'Is this why we are doing this?'" A deep satisfaction came when the teacher realized later in the school year that her white and black pupils were about even scholastically, and that the white children had not been hurt by the transition.

"I think about that now," she told me. "I know that if integration had not come when it did—or sometime—these children would have gone right on in the same old way of not being prepared."

It was under such conditions that the federal government moved to require that the new high court decision be obeyed. It might be logically asked why there was such a long delay in enforcement of the Supreme Court school decision. The guideline set by the court was compliance "with all deliberate speed," and that inevitably permitted delaying tactics. The courts and the federal government exercised patience so as to permit the great social change to develop gradually, if possible. But the insistence on compliance, if gradual and patient, was never absent.

With the cautious movement toward desegregation in public secondary and elementary education, ambitious and bright black students began to apply for admission to institutions of public higher education. So it was that, after months of legal sparring, the United States Supreme Court on October 10, 1955, ordered the University of Alabama to admit its first black students, Autherine Lucy and Polly Anne Myers Hudson, both Birmingham women.

Demonstrations, wild and almost out of control, erupted on the big campus at Tuscaloosa. After three days of university attendance, Autherine Lucy, the only one of the two who made the actual enrollment attempt, was suspended "for her own safety," according to the university. She escaped from the campus through an angry crowd by lying on the floor of a state patrol car. The black student sued in court for readmission, but her testimony backfired. On February 29, she was expelled for "outrageous" charges that she made against the university during the hearing. No one sought to reverse the expulsion.

According to a study by the authoritative *Southern School News* in May 1957, three years after the Supreme Court school decision, 685 school districts in nine states had begun or completed the desegregation process out of 3,700 school districts in the seventeen states that had statutory segregation in 1954. But legislatures in eleven states had adopted more than 130 pieces of pro-segregation legislation. In Georgia the State Board of Regents, the policy-making body for the University System, changed entrance regulations at the University of Georgia Law School to require character references from alumni and public officials in the applicant's home county. This rule change came after a black graduate student sought to enter the law school.

Marvin Griffin, who was then governor of Georgia, asked the state legislature in the fall of 1955 to pass a law prohibiting Georgia football teams from playing against teams with blacks in the lineup. Students at Georgia Tech, a state university, staged a loud demonstration in front of the governor's mansion in Atlanta to protest the governor's proposed ban on Tech meeting Pittsburgh, which had black players, in the 1956 Sugar Bowl. The state Board of Regents, controlling body for the universities, rejected the governor's proposal before it reached the floor of the legislature. Georgia Tech met Pitt in the Sugar Bowl and was beaten 7-0 before a crowd of eighty thousand.

And so it went, this testing match with the federal courts, with every one wondering when the feds would start really grading the test papers—and knowing it would be soon.

In the spring of 1957, Arkansas appeared to be moving with apparent willingness toward desegregation of public schools in the fall. State school officials simply noted that local districts were autonomous on all school matters. Little Rock, the capital city, won a "good faith compliance" federal court test of a gradual desegregation plan, and local school officials announced publicly that the city would proceed with high school integration in September. Yet, it was here in Little Rock at a schoolhouse door that the first real test of the government's determination to enforce a court order took place.

Although sections of Arkansas were all-white, and remained so through the years, the state as a whole could not have been labeled a militant holdout against integration. Several cities had quietly integrated without difficulty, and without interference from Governor Orval Faubus. The governor's son attended a non-segregated college.

There was little reaction when the Little Rock Board of Education on May 25 decided to obey federal district court orders to desegregate Central High School. At that time, Central was one of four high schools in Little Rock. The others were Dunbar (for blacks), Horace Mann, and Hall. No white pupils had entered Horace Mann (for blacks), and no black pupils had entered Hall (for whites). They would have been eligible to do so under a September 1956 order from Federal Judge Ronald N. Davies that all Little Rock school district senior high schools were to be desegregated "forthwith."

The Little Rock school board appealed to adults and students for acceptance of the court's order, stressing that the board had no alternative but to comply with the directive. Nine black pupils, all seniors, were due to enroll at Central—and it should be noted that this step had been anticipated calmly and publicly for two years, even before the court orders made the act mandatory. The state government knew every important detail of the plans. Yet, on the night before the opening of school, Governor Faubus suddenly announced he had received secret information that a small group of white racial extremists would disrupt peaceful integration of Central High.

Faubus called out a token force of state National Guardsmen "to maintain or restore the peace and good order of this community," as the governor put it. The school board asked black pupils to delay their entry until the "dilemma" of troops on the campus was "legally solved." Appearing on local television the evening of September 3, the governor said: "I must state here in all sincerity that it is my opinion, yes, even a conviction, that it will not be possible to preserve order and protect the lives and property of citizens if forcible integration is carried out tomorrow in the schools of this community."

On the opening of the fall term the next day, there were no blacks at Central—only white students being treated to the unusual sight of state troopers patrolling the halls. The nine blacks had been met some distance from the campus by members of the Arkansas National Guard and turned away. The governor insisted the action was "to preserve law and order." On September 20, Federal Judge Ronald Davies ruled that the governor had not used the National Guard to preserve law and order, as he had stated. The court forbade the governor and his Guard to interfere with integration at Central High. In his order, the federal judge said: "The chief executive of Little Rock [Mayor Woodrow Mann] has stated that the Little Rock police have not had a single case of interracial violence in regard to this situation." He said firmly that "in an organized society, there can be nothing but ultimate confusion and chaos" if court decrees are not obeyed, "whatever the pretense."

The governor's lawyers responded by walking out of the federal hearing, but Faubus removed the state troops, and Little Rock police took up their positions. Faubus complained that the federal government was "cramming integration down our throats" but would not help the state "handle the enforcement."

On Monday morning, September 24, eight of the nine black pupils returned to school and slipped into the building by a side door. A crowd of more than one thousand whites went wild outside. The black pupils were taken home in two heavily guarded police cars.

President Eisenhower, who had dealt cautiously with the Little Rock case, including a personal session he had initiated with Faubus at the White House, now moved swiftly although with reluctance. On the afternoon of September 24, the president federalized the Arkansas National Guard, which meant that the Guard was now in the U.S. Army and subject to court martial. The president also sent twelve hundred paratroopers of the 101st Airborne Division to the Central High campus.

On the morning of September 25, high school students were treated to a sight they would long remember: screaming demonstrators on the Central

High schoolyard, soldiers with fixed bayonets, network television. In the midst of this, all nine black pupils arrived on the campus in an army staff car and walked into Central High School through the front entrance, escorted by twenty soldiers of the 101st Airborne. Army troops dispersed crowds and restored order. The black pupils were in school.

Thus, the fall school term began, and one of the first assembly speakers was the man in charge of all those soldiers—Major General Edwin A. Walker, a decorated veteran of World War II.

"You have nothing to fear from my soldiers, and no one will interfere with your coming, going, or your peaceful pursuit of your studies," he told the assembled students. "However," he added, "I would be less than honest if I failed to tell you that I intend to use all means necessary to prevent any interference with the execution of your school board's plan."

None of Little Rock's four high schools opened for the 1958 session, on orders of the governor. He urged parents to enroll their children in private schools that were to be partially financed by state revenue in the amount of $600,000 per year. Again the Supreme Court stepped in, ordering the Little Rock school board to make public schools available to pupils who desired to attend. The decision stopped a proposal to lease the closed Little Rock school buildings to a corporation that would operate private, segregated schools. Relatively routine school life resumed in the summer of 1959.

After normalcy had returned to Central High, I went back to Little Rock on assignment by UPI to assess the progress of desegregation. Jess Matthews, who was principal of Central at the time of the crisis and still held that office, told me: "When our school was closed for a year, pupils and parents realized just how much it meant to have it open. There are very few incidents any more."

Recalling the days when troops were on the Central High campus and could be viewed by pupils from the classrooms, the principal observed that "the thing people don't realize is that even at the worst time, when the troops were all over the place, we were still teaching classes. There was a lot of shoving and some fighting in the halls, but the teachers never once lost control of their classes."

In those early years of school desegregation, I heard it said in cities all over the South that the children, had they been isolated from adult influence, would have made the big social adjustment with comparative ease. The talk they heard at home, the daily bombardment of statements and directives from public officials, and the nightly news on television—it was too much for young minds to cope with, and the youngsters reacted with intense excitement that often turned quickly to anger. On occasion, I heard the saltiest of profanity from the lips of very young elementary school pupils—just as I heard the same torrents from the lips of their mothers. Invariably, however, when the uniformed officers and troops departed and the story no longer dominated the news, a large majority of public elementary and high schools in the segregated states accepted the fact of integration with no more than a few days of shouting and shoving in the halls.

Washington, D.C., under mandate of President Eisenhower to make the city "the most integrated in America," led the way in removing all racial barriers in the classrooms. District schools, like many others that were new to mixed enrollments, saw pupil achievement records decline sharply for several years. Dedicated teachers and new learning programs designed to help under-educated pupils served to bring these schools back to and above national average.

In Atlanta, the children of Dr. and Mrs. Martin Luther King, Jr., were enrolled without obstacle or incident in public schools. Dr. M. L. (Daddy) King Sr., the children's grandfather, observed the event for two of the children, Yolanda and Martin, in the shade of a tree on the schoolground. I found him there, quietly confident that school integration would soon become a normal way of life in the South.

By 1960, only six years after the high court ordered the start of school desegregation, the South's public schools opened routinely for the fall term. It was the first time since 1954 that there were no reported racial incidents in the schools.

Charlayne Hunter (left) and Hamilton Holmes walk down a sidewalk in Athens, Georgia, en route to the University of Georgia registrar's office to become the first blacks to enroll at the state-supported institution. They arrived shortly after the registrar opened on January 9, 1961, armed with court orders to ensure their admission. Photo: © Bettmann-Corbis

CHAPTER 3

1961–Passing the Test: Integrating the University of Georgia

"And so each venture is a new beginning . . . For us, there is only the trying. The rest is not our business."

—Thomas Stearns Eliot

In the first years of school desegregation in the South, there was interminable argument as to whether it was best to start the transition in the earliest years of a child's life or at the college level. In some states there was no pattern, leaving a difficult process at both ends of the scale. The Universities of Georgia, Mississippi, and Alabama were hit by the stiffest opposition to change at the upper level, not because of the institutions but because of the state governments that controlled them.

Join me in the year 1961 on the campus of the University of Georgia.

Town and Gown merge in Athens, Georgia—in 1961 a busy seat of county government in its own right, even without a big university. The town was especially busy on Saturdays when farmers came in from the countryside to buy and sell, when it was tax time, or when court was in session. The university was like another city, but it was tolerated because it produced both money and fame for Athens. Until 1961, the noisiest demonstrations in town celebrated victories of the Georgia Bulldogs football team. On one side of the campus, town is just across the street from The Varsity, where students and townspeople mingle for fast food.

In the fall of 1960, two black students, both well qualified academically, applied for admission to the University of Georgia. Under state law at that time, they could not be admitted, for the legislature had done nothing to bring universities under the 1954 Supreme Court school desegregation decision. The U.S. District Court ruled otherwise, ordering the university to enroll Charlayne Hunter, a transfer student from Wayne State University in Detroit, and Hamilton Holmes, transferring from Morehouse College in Atlanta, Georgia, at the opening of the winter term.

Governor Ernest Vandiver, playing for time while the legislature fiddled with the necessity to change state laws, refused to budge. The university, its hands tied by the state law, helplessly waited for the inevitable collision of state and federal power.

The week after Christmas of 1960 the press corps moved into the Holiday Inn motel in Athens and spent the week chasing rumors, meeting university people, and getting familiar with the campus. Tensions in town and on the campus grew steadily in anticipation of coming events.

One cold night, the fire alarm downtown went off with a terrible screech. Reporters, suspicious that the alarm could mean a black home being put to the torch, cleared the motel parking lot before the fire engine got out of sight. A long line of news cars trailed the equipment into the countryside. A farmer, who had called the fire department to a small blaze in his hay barn, probably never understood why he had attracted three national television networks with all their equipment, wire services, and an assortment of other national media correspondents.

During the week before the scheduled integration, state lawyers took one final defensive step, appearing before U.S. District Judge W. A. Bootle in Macon, Georgia. They won a delay in the earlier desegregation order, but it was a very temporary delay; within hours Elbert Tuttle, chief judge of the U.S. Court of Appeals, reversed Bootle's decision. The die was cast.

On Monday morning, January 9, Athens was tense but quiet. State police were in evidence, and even more troopers were garrisoned near the city. National Guardsmen were moved into the Athens armory. But troopers and Guardsmen took no part in the impending crisis, leaving it to the Athens city police force to take the brunt of any trouble on the city streets. At this stage, there was no indication that the governor would attempt to thwart registration of the black students.

Shortly before 8 a.m. on the 9th, Charlayne Hunter and Hamilton Holmes were brought onto the campus by university officials, in separate cars and through back entrances. They were greeted by reporters and a small group of curious students. Hunter was assigned a small apartment with kitchen in Myers Hall on the university's famous "Ag Hill." Holmes was housed in town until a room became available on the campus. The black students were formally registered without incident. They were escorted through a side door of the registrar's office, disappointing a large crowd of students waiting at another entrance.

If some segments of society thought of these two students as "guinea pigs" of the integration movement, they never thought of themselves as such. They had their eyes on the stars and could not see the clouds. Throughout their university experience, they approached their education with dignity and a determination to succeed.

Hunter and Holmes had been schoolmates at Atlanta's Turner High, a black school. She had her dream of a journalism career; his was to be a physician. Holmes often thought of attending the University of Georgia as the pinnacle of ambition, knowing all the while that its doors were closed to him. When his father, who had been instrumental in getting Atlanta golf courses desegregated, and a few other black leaders suggested that Hamilton apply at one of the state's public all-white universities, he jumped at the chance. Georgia was his obvious choice. The same group of senior blacks then approached Charlayne Hunter who was attending Wayne State University.

There was quiet before the storm on that first Monday at the University of Georgia, but that night student emotions built up. Shouting crowds roamed the streets of Athens, blocking traffic, and vowing unspecified trouble for the black students. But so far, the demonstrators had no visible target for their wrath; their antics only bore watching. The university position was to keep a low profile. Dean of Students Joe Williams and Dean of Men James Tate were the highest ranking officials on the scene.

Tate, who had the build of a college athlete and a stentorian voice, gave the student excitement time to wear down and successfully encouraged the crowd to go to their dorms. Athens was quiet before midnight.

By Tuesday, however, agitation was again evident. The word was that a big demonstration would take place that night on a city street bordering the campus. A huge throng turned out. Tate had more trouble than the night before, but again he managed to keep things under control. There still was no visible target, and that helped.

On Wednesday, although university officials expressed their first serious concern that students were getting out of hand, the black students were taken to their classes without incident.

Reporters and television crews easily discovered the class schedules of the black students and camped outside their buildings. A wire service reporter, not long out of college herself, slipped into Charlayne Hunter's classroom under guise of being a coed. A photographer also got in.

As undergraduate classes dismissed, thousands of students hit the main campus almost at the same time. The television crews were a great attraction, and crowds swarmed to them like moths to a flame. It was my first experience observing the power of television. It was like a studio show where an assistant warms up an audience before the star comes on, coaching the crowd on cues to cheer. While awaiting the appearance of Hunter and Holmes, reporters did student reaction interviews, moving among the crowd. It was not long before television reporters were asking: "What are you going to say to them when they come out?"

"Nigger, go home."

The cameras were rolling—sound on film: "Nigger, go home."

The film was on flights to New York before noon, in plenty of time for the evening news shows. The nation, and thousands of university students who had not witnessed the day's events, were stunned by chants of "Nigger, go home" on their television screens.

That Wednesday night, the Georgia basketball team, the Southeastern Conference leader, was defeated 89-80 by arch rival Georgia Tech in the campus field house. Tempers were high, resulting from some controversial calls by the referee. Spectators surged out of the building and onto the campus.

A loud but still-manageable demonstration, not unlike a college rally, was in progress outside Charlayne Hunter's dormitory near the edge of the campus. The basketball crowd carried their indignation right to the heart of the gathering.

By now there was another factor. Students had been joined by a small but militant band of white adults. One was Calvin Craig, grand dragon of the Georgia Ku Klux Klans. I watched him and his followers (not in Klan regalia) moving through the crowd, passing out white supremacy propaganda. This group understood how to convert a demonstration into a mob.

Adding to the confusion were the totally inadequate police measures for dealing with the escalating trouble. The huge campus was state property, and its security depended on university security personnel. Athens city police, who in the past had encountered problems in crossing the line from city to state property, had a firm rule in effect: Let the state protect its own property. The city would not send police onto the campus. Further complicating things, state police, who could have reached the crisis zone in minutes, stayed away. No barrier, not even a hedge, separated city street from state university, and so the crowds roamed at will, never deterred by the small Athens police force or the smaller university security detail. Rocks and bottles were soon flying.

A television camera's lights were smashed. Car windows were broken. City police were harassed. An unsuccessful entry was attempted into Charlayne Hunter's dormitory, and a window was broken in her ground floor suite. Tear gas and fire hoses were used for the first time to stop the crowd that was still on city property.

With the disturbance turning ugly, university officials decided the lives of the two black students were in danger, and they were suspended "until it is safe and practical for them to return." State police finally showed up to remove them to places of safekeeping in the city. Word passed through the crowd that victory was won—the blacks were gone. By midnight Wednesday all was calm.

On Saturday morning, U.S. District Judge W. A. Bootle, sitting in Macon, ordered the university to return the black students to their classes on Monday and directed the state of Georgia to provide all necessary protection. The court held that a small group of white students, encouraged by white adults, had caused Wednesday night's riot.

The university administration, anguished by events of the week, was determined there would be no repeat the following week. The governor and state police were kept informed and were asked for cooperation in the university's planned course of action.

This was the plan:

- Rule 1 The black students will be re-admitted.
- Rule 2–The university campus will be off limits to anyone having no legitimate business there.
- Rule 3–The education process for Charlayne Hunter, Hamilton Holmes and all other students will not be interrupted by further disturbances.
- Rule 4–Student violators of good-conduct rules will be disciplined, suspended, or expelled.
- Rule 5–Something has to be done about news coverage.

The last rule was a sticky one. The university was state property, and therefore public property. How far could the university go in exercising direction over the media?

The solution was a simple but classic case that was followed in the future by other institutions faced with the same dilemma. In those turbulent days, some universities, anticipating problems later on, sent observers to places like Athens, much as a college football coach scouts the next week's opponent.

Reporters were invited—not ordered, invited—by the University of Georgia administration to a meeting on Saturday afternoon. Problems of the week were reviewed. The university's plan for the following week was discussed. Then the news people were asked—not ordered, asked—to have their own meeting, with a university representative present, and agree on a code of self-discipline in covering this story.

Acquiescence was not immediate. Some reporters sounded off on censorship, freedom of the press, the public's right to know all that was going on. "Fine," the administration said in effect, "We'll help you tell the story."

After the speeches were over, mutual agreement on what should be done was reached—quietly, intelligently, and responsibly: Reporters would not "stake out" university buildings where the black students were in class.

They would not follow them about the campus, nor try to contact them for interviews and reaction on their experiences each day. The university would cooperate by providing weekly interviews with the black students. There would be regular briefings with the news media. The meeting ended in a spirit of mutual cooperation.

The next week, Charlayne Hunter and Hamilton Holmes were returned to their classes. There was no further trouble. The state police detail in Athens remained nearby. City officers had things well in hand. Within a few months, extra troopers were removed.

Whether the plan devised by the university pleased the news media, or whether it was considered a violation of freedom of the press, can be argued. But it worked, and it became something of a model.

The UPI bureaus in Atlanta and New York were notified of the press meeting with the university, and all other developments. They had my report that I was one of the first to accept the "new style" of reporting by news people. They endorsed that. All they wanted was the story in detail. Big deal! How was that to be handled? It was handled in a most unusual way.

I was walking in the early morning along one of the campus roads, wondering how I could discover which entrance the two black students would be using—and without breaking a single official rule. As I was deep in thought, someone called my name from a group on the other side of the road. The call was from an official with whom I had become acquainted earlier; he had been very interested in news of other campuses.

"I'm sorry, can't stop," I said while walking on.

"Get over here!" my friend ordered. "Get in the car; we are going to town to pick up the boy. Thought you would like to go."

And so we went to town, picked up Hamilton at his "safe house" residence and headed back to the campus. I had a thirty-minute talk with this student, but got little to use. He was calm but a bit nervous. He just wanted to get started with his long-delayed entry. (I was grateful for having learned an important point for reporters—get to know as many as possible of those you deal with.)

Although the two black students became regular undergraduates and performed well academically, they were never accepted into the mainstream of student life. Holmes told a reporter that he did not eat in the university dining hall, did not study in the library, did not use the gymnasium, and did not enter the snack bar. He said that no white student ever visited him and he never visited a white student. Charlayne Hunter told of receiving many letters of encouragement but said she had no white friends. "I look around and I don't see anybody else," she said.

Following her graduation, the university's first black coed, by then Charlayne Hunter-Galt, became highly successful as a television journalist. She appeared as a regular member of the *McNeil-Lehrer News Hour*, produced by Public Broadcasting Service (PBS), expertly handling the most sensitive news events in the calm and probing manner of a good professional reporter. As I watched television during her assignment years later in South Africa—where the racial turmoil far surpassed that in the American South— I saw her gently seeking information from all sides, sorting out the facts of a very complex story. In the memory flashback, I saw a still-shy young woman challenging a great state university where an old segregation tradition was then almost a religion.

Following his graduation from the University of Georgia, Hamilton Holmes enrolled in the Emory University Medical School in Atlanta, its first black student. He became a prominent neurosurgeon whose patients numbered almost as many whites as blacks. A white patient for whom Holmes performed delicate and successful surgery and sat by her bedside to comfort, called him "my wonderful man."

In 1983 Holmes was elected to the board of trustees of the University of Georgia Foundation, a private non-profit corporation that manages gifts to the university. He said at the time he hoped to help other minority citizens benefit from the university.

Holmes told an interviewer that he would like to be remembered as someone who had "aspirations to be the best in everything I tried to do."

James Meredith (right) and U.S. Marshal Joseph P. McShane (center) are turned away from the entrance to the University of Mississippi, in Oxford, by Lt. Gov. Paul Johnson (left) on September 26, 1962. Meredith later became the first black student admitted to Ole Miss. Photo: United Press International

CHAPTER 4

1962-1964–The Battle of Ole Miss

"O God, give us serenity to accept what cannot be changed, courage to change what should be changed, and wisdom to distinguish the one from the other."

—Prayer of Reinhold Niebuhr

Oxford, Mississippi, is the home of novelist William Faulkner. In the fall of 1961, not long after Faulkner received the Nobel Prize for Literature, nor long before his death on February 27, 1962, I walked between the rows of ancient oaks that lined the approach to his antebellum home at the edge of town for an interview. At the time he was Mississippi's best-known literary figure and was often sought after for opinions about life in his state. He talked with me of changes coming to his world and how the people of Mississippi were not ready for it, but had better get ready.

At the time of our meeting, Oxford was so thoroughly segregated that one outside corner of the Lafayette County courthouse property was reserved for blacks, where they could sit and visit in segregated comfort.

Writing in *Life* magazine, Faulkner advised civil rights groups to give the Southerner time in which to get his breath and become better informed about integration. He wrote that he was against segregation or integration by compulsion. He echoed those sentiments during our talk, there in a parlor that reflected much more of the past than the present—much less the future of his state. He felt that some things should never change and that it would require time and patience for other change to come and be accepted. The whole atmosphere of his place reflected that sentiment.

William Faulkner was no crusader for change. He locked himself in his big musty house and wrote of white sharecroppers, of misery, and struggle. With or without his permission, however, change was moving in on his world. It arrived in Oxford in late September 1962.

"It's going to be a long night."

The main entrance to the University of Mississippi—the treasured "Ole Miss" of many generations of Mississippians—is across Hilgard Bridge spanning railroad tracks that border the Oxford campus. A narrow roadway circles a tree-shaded lawn locally identified as The Grove. The road slopes up the hill to the Lyceum, the stately old administration building that stands sentinel over the campus and the town beyond.

James Meredith, veteran of nine years in the U.S. Air Force, twenty-nine-year-old son of a black Koskiusko, Mississippi, farmer, came home determined to break the segregation barrier at Ole Miss. In the military service, he had done academic work at six colleges. In 1961, while attending Jackson State College, an all-black institution at the state capital, he applied to enter the University of Mississippi.

Meredith's application was denied, and there followed sixteen months of legal effort that culminated in a federal court order to permit his admission to the university. Governor Ross Barnett said "No!" and the battle lines were drawn again between state and federal authority. The feds reacted with strength.

It was a strange route of academic admission for Meredith. It began at the Memphis, Tennessee, Naval Air Station. There, he met his escorts to Ole Miss—430 U.S. marshals.

Around noon on September 30, a Sunday of Indian summer beauty in the South, Meredith was flown to Oxford in one of four transport planes used to move him to the campus, along with 260 of the marshals. Army trucks transported 170 other marshals the seventy miles from Memphis to Oxford.

The little Oxford airport looked like a frontline military air base. The several times I was there in the hours and days ahead, Air Force and Border Patrol planes filled almost every spot. The U.S. government set up its own control tower to monitor the numerous takeoffs and landings.

James Meredith was checked into a two-bedroom, second-floor dormitory apartment at the university. This was not special treatment; the room was needed for U.S. marshals who would live with him literally every hour of the day and night during that senior year.

Marshals donned flak jackets and canisters of tear gas. They took up positions at the Lyceum and waited for developments. They were augmented by a detail of state troopers. Meredith turned in early, in preparation for his registration the next morning.

University registrars, caught as others had been in the power struggle between state and federal governments, were helpless to do other than follow the federal mandate: register James Meredith. Others would have to decide if he stayed.

News that the black student was actually on the campus was quickly broadcast through the university community and to the town and countryside nearby. As night fell, the columned Lyceum, whose name came from the gymnasium where Aristotle taught philosophy in ancient Athens, stood at the top of The Grove as the paradigm of all that Mississippi represented.

Before it was over, more than 350 journalists covered this one event—an incredible number then; not so now with many hundreds of news people concentrating on a special story. I checked into the Journalism building, halfway down the hill from the Lyceum, with a small and, I must say, courageous crew of reporters and photographers. The Journalism building was well-equipped for that period, had its own presses, adequate desk space for anyone who had time to type, and, more importantly, bathroom facilities. The journalism department was helpful, and the J students on hand were understandably excited. Here they were in the midst of the biggest story of their lives.

Soon after dark, groups of students, just back from a football game, began gathering before the Lyceum for what started out as noisy fun—although from the beginning there was an undercurrent of resentment. More offensive than the arrival of a black student on the campus was the presence of federal authority. And here it was, dressed in flak jackets, surrounding their Lyceum.

After about an hour, the students began throwing lighted cigarettes at the marshals and Mississippi state troopers guarding the Lyceum. A rain of pebbles, scooped up from the campus drive, followed—spattering the hard hats of the officers. But they calmly stood their ground. Had the university been able to limit the demonstrators to students, the exercise may have worn itself out with shouting, name-calling, and a few rocks and bottles. It was not possible, for this wide-open campus was an invitation to involvement by outsiders. Radio and television were giving the populace at large a play-by-play description of the mounting student protest.

Outsiders drifted onto the campus shortly after 7 p.m., singly, in pairs, and in groups—gaunt, hard-faced white adults. It was chilling to watch their appearance on the already-tense scene. They carried lengths of boards studded with nails, jagged bottles, some filled with gasoline with soaked wicks sticking out, and buckets of broken bricks from a university building site just off campus.

By now, the visitors had mingled with students and were organizing an attack on the Lyceum. Up ahead, a mob was in the making. The crowd commandeered a bulldozer and a fire truck—brought in to hose down the demonstrators—and were soon driven wildly back and forth before the thin line of marshals encircling the Lyceum. Rocks began raining on their hard hats and bouncing off their flak jackets. The state troopers were right in the fray.

A breakthrough by the mob appeared imminent when the order was passed among the federal agents to begin using tear gas. The opening barrage caught state troopers standing between marshals and students. A number fell, some hit in the chest by discharged canisters. The state force soon withdrew in disgust, leaving the situation to the feds—"physically overpowered by the federal government," Governor Barnett put it. When the state police left, it was open season on the federal force at the Lyceum; all semblance of law and order disappeared.

The first clouds of acrid smoke drove back the aggressors, but they were far from finished. Spewing tear gas canisters were picked up hot from the ground and hurled back into the midst of the marshals. Again and again, the federal force was assailed. The injured dropped out to be replaced by reinforcements. Before that night ended, more than 160 marshals were injured, including twenty-two shot.

Taking it all in on one of my trips up the hill through the milling crowd, it was difficult almost beyond belief to realize this was happening in America—or to maintain an objective correspondent's perspective. It was like a bad dream: middle-aged men exhorting young students to attack the Lyceum guards; swirling tear gas smoke providing an eerie veil over the scene. Momentarily, I was overcome by the thought that I was witnessing the end of a civilization. I stood in the confusion and wept, thanking the darkness for keeping the secret. When the melancholy mood passed, I went on toward the hilltop Lyceum.

About 10 p.m., we heard the spit of rifle fire. Snipers had found a way to the upper floors of at least two buildings and were firing at random toward the Lyceum. After awhile, the shooting subsided. There were two deaths that night. Paul Guihard, a reporter for Agence France-Presse, was found near a dormitory far from the riot, shot from behind at close range. Ray Gunter, a jukebox repairman who had wandered onto the campus to watch the action, was killed by a shot as he crossed the campus bridge at the foot of The Grove.

It was hard to believe that James Meredith, the subject and object of all this, was sleeping peacefully in a dorm room nearby. For myself, I envied Meredith's comfort. By midnight my colleagues and I were bone-weary, but adrenalin power kept us going. On one shuttle trip from the Journalism building to The Grove I passed Leon Daniel, one of our finest reporters. "Be careful, it's mean out there," he said as he disappeared into the darkness.

I had spent the entire previous day getting ready for what was now happening. This night seemed to last forever. In 1957 United Press foreign editor Joe Alex Morris wrote a book titled *Deadline Every Minute*, a very accurate picture of the wire service organization's work. Dailies and magazines, and even radio and television, had their deadlines; but ours happened every minute because somewhere in the world some client wanted to know what was happening in Oxford.

Occasionally during the night, food would appear in the J building, and I ate gratefully and without paying. Absence of a bed or a cot presented no problem because there was no time for sleep. Yet, some of the finest reporting comes from such pressure-packed assignments. My own experience was not unusual, but I have thought since how some internal mechanism causes the juices to flow with accelerated effectiveness in times of abject weariness or distress. During a brief lull that night, sometime after midnight, a call came from the UPI office in Atlanta. A client paper in South America—the great *La Prensa* of Argentina—wanted a two-thousand-word reprise on the night's events, told in the words of a correspondent on the scene.

"I can't do it; I'm dead," I protested. But it was done. It required taking a deep breath and dictating. I learned later that the story went out to the South American paper just as it was dictated.

Rest would come later—about twenty-four hours later. In a building a few hundred yards from the riot, Assistant U.S. Attorney General Nicholas deB. Katzenbach, Attorney General Robert Kennedy's deputy, kept his boss and President John F. Kennedy informed of the worsening situation. He reported that the marshals, unable to fight back except with tear gas, could be overrun.

The president acted without further delay. He ordered the Mississippi National Guard federalized and sent to the university. One of the National Guardsmen called to Oxford was the governor's son. The statute used to call up the troops dated to May 2, 1792. George Washington first used it to put down a 1794 whiskey rebellion in Pennsylvania where booze makers rioted against a federal excise tax.

In an open telegram to the state of Mississippi and the nation, President Kennedy said: "If this country should ever reach the point where any man or any group of men by force or threat of force should long defy the commands of our court and our Constitution, then no law would stand free from doubt, no judge would be sure of his writ, and no citizen would be safe from his neighbor."

Then the president sent this message to the university students: "You have a new opportunity to show that you are men of patriotism and integrity, for the most effective means of upholding the law is not the state policemen or the marshals, or the National Guard. It is you. It lies within your courage to accept those laws with which you disagree, as well as those with which you agree."

So soon, so soon would both JFK and Robert, his young brother, be cut down by assassin's bullets—the president on a highway motorcade in Dallas in 1963, his brother while being escorted through the basement of a Los Angeles hotel in 1968. The agony of race, or any expression of it, was exposing America to its worst.

It was too late for words to be effective; every new appeal from the government seemed to aggravate the situation. Most of the undergraduate students—men and women—who had started this night half in boisterous fun, reacted with fright now. Many left the scene. The hard-liners and the outsiders remained to the bitter end. Ed Meek, who became director of public relations for the university years later, but was then a staff photographer who had just graduated, recalled:

"I was scared . . . Not only was I afraid for my safety; I knew that a grand institution was being destroyed, or at least severely damaged. It hurt me; it made me mad. But I didn't comprehend everything then. I didn't know what a catastrophe it was. It got out of control."

Federalized National Guard troops came first, followed swiftly by elements of the 101st Airborne Division of the U.S. Army. It was now past 2 a.m. and the battle of the Lyceum was still in progress.

I looked toward the town and watched the airborne troops roll onto the campus in a long line of jeeps, the low-slung lights of their vehicles shining like big fireflies in the dark. I looked the other way, up through The Grove, and saw through the mist, the mob, and the thin line of federal marshals, and the Lyceum, brightly lit.

Ed Meek: "By morning, 3,000 troops came in here. A C-130 landed every five minutes. The planes barely stopped. The bellies opened and the people popped out. Soon, there were 30-caliber machineguns and foxholes around the campus."

The troops were businesslike. They sealed the campus; they swept The Grove clear of rioters; they rescued the marshals. By the time they finished, it was dawn. Still standing was the thin line of federal marshals, and the

Lyceum, its white wooden columns pock-marked with bullet holes. The fumes of tear gas would remain until Oxford had a good rain.

On the morning of October 2, James Meredith, who still insisted he had slept through most of the disturbance, registered and began classes. His first class was Colonial American History. In the spring of 1963, Meredith graduated in political science, the first of his race to have a degree from proud Ole Miss. It had required more than three thousand soldiers and had cost the federal government almost five million dollars to uphold the law that gave him the right to enroll. A detail of five hundred marshals was assigned to his case until he graduated.

In a reflective mood following his graduation, Meredith wrote a letter to *The Justice*, the student newspaper at Brandeis University: "We will have to find a formula that will permit the Negro to gain pride and dignity, and yet leave the whites with an assurance that their security will not be jeopardized.

"We must find a common denominator that will permit both races to work together in finding an answer to our problems; and, more important, we must find a way to work together in actually solving our problems. I feel that the time has arrived to find a new pattern for dealing with the race question.

"I feel confident that a new pattern will be discovered, and I believe that Mississippi may well take the initiative and blot out its blackened past, and proceed on to an enlightened phase of race relations and human dignity."

Finally, I had an old belief corroborated, that Mississippi, despite its racial feelings, would make peace with that issue and carry the state to greatness. With race settled by state policy, Mississippi began to thrive financially. A more progressive government wooed Northern business with tax benefits leading to many more jobs. Earlier, I was laughed out of the conversation for such a prediction.

By October 6, only one week after the agony at the Lyceum, the Ole Miss story was off the front pages. On that day, I noted that the *New York Times* used part of page 1 for a two-column headline: "Baby bottles needn't be warm, research at Belleview indicates."

The next time Meredith came into the news was two years later when he embarked on a private, one-man 220-mile "March Against Fear" from Memphis, Tennessee, to Jackson, Mississippi. After all the racial turmoil that had been packed into those several years, Meredith's march seemed to draw little attention.

On the afternoon of June 6, 1966, I was working in my garden in Atlanta when I was called to the telephone. It was the UPI office. Another wire service had reported that James Meredith had been ambushed and killed on the road to Jackson.

As I drove to the news bureau at breakneck speed, my thoughts raced with the implications of this event. It could be the spark that would touch off a new round of wild racial trouble. The only thing I could think to do was to confirm what had happened. But how?

At the office, I found that they had the name of the hospital and had learned Meredith was taken to surgery. Even as I dialed the hospital number, I realized how fruitless it would be to get the information desk and nothing more. Waiting for an answer from the hospital switchboard, a daring idea came.

"Ring surgery, please," I requested the operator in a tone I hoped would produce results.

I heard a phone ringing, and presently a male voice came on the line. "This is surgery," he said. Quickly, I got to the point. I had to know if James Meredith was dead.

"He is very much alive. I should know. I am the doctor working on him now. He has superficial wounds."

It took less than thirty seconds to kill the rumor on the news wires that went to the Mississippi media.

In 1983, the University of Mississippi quietly observed the twentieth anniversary of the James Meredith experience—and two decades of routine admission of black students to Ole Miss. By then, about 9 percent of the 9,412 students were black, and on the increase. It would be inaccurate to suggest that Meredith's admission and graduation at the University of Mississippi ended all racial discrimination in the state's education institutions, but the spin-offs from that one event can hardly be measured. All up and down the line of school systems in the state, and into countless black homes, the word was passed that finally it was worth going to school because up the road from some little community school was the University of Mississippi, and Ole Miss was looking for bright black students.

I thought of that old black man I had met on the Delta and how he had dreamed of a day like this.

Brigadier General Henry V. Graham, officer in charge of federalized Alabama National Guard units, salutes Alabama Governor George C. Wallace at the University of Alabama in Tuscaloosa on June 16, 1963. Graham informed Wallace that troops had entered the campus to enforce a court order directing the university to admit black students Vivian J. Malone and James Hood. Photo: © Bettmann-Corbis

CHAPTER 5

1963–University of Alabama Integrates despite Wallace

"Listen to me, children, put on your marching shoes"

—Dr. Martin Luther King, Jr.

*"Democracy is still upon its trial. The civic genius of our people
is its only bulwark."*   —William James

Shortly after he became U.S. attorney general, Robert Kennedy was invited by a student organization to visit the University of Alabama at the height of local reaction against his own and the president's stand on desegregation. Kennedy was urged by advisers not to consider the trip, but he insisted on going to Tuscaloosa.

When Kennedy arrived at the huge Alabama basketball arena with Ethel, his wife, the place was packed with a standup crowd of boisterous students. A platform had been constructed that jutted out over the arena floor. The Kennedys entered from a ramp that extended to a back corridor of the arena.

The attorney general spoke, or attempted to speak, for almost twenty minutes concerning the necessity to obey laws and court decisions, whether or not they were popular. He was interrupted numerous times by catcalls and boos. By the end of his remarks, it must have been obvious to Kennedy that he had not put over his point. His audience was definitely not friendly. Standing there watching, I saw it would have been easy for him to gracefully and safely exit with Ethel the way they came in.

That was not Bobby Kennedy's style; he never ran away from a fight—whether he was right or wrong. This time he led Ethel to the edge of the platform, which stood at least four feet from the gymnasium floor. Grasping her hand, they jumped together into the midst of the student body. That simple, courageous act broke the spell, and students rushed to shake Kennedy's hand and talk. This was one of those unexpected factors that helped pave the way for student acceptance of integration at the University of Alabama. It was not long in coming.

The university's approach to the coming crisis was a model of planning. In part it was intelligently observing what had gone before and willingness to go after facts. The staff was eager to talk with news reporters who had come to Tuscaloosa off a long trail of experience. From all the evidence, decisions were made.

Daily made aware of the state's official and emotional determination to keep the university segregated, the institution nonetheless quietly began its preparations, based on its research and scouting activity. What were the problems other areas and other institutions encountered when blacks came knocking at their segregated doors? How were the problems handled? What were the mistakes? Who was in charge? Alabama had time, and used it wisely. There were ample case histories for study, in and out of education:

- The 381-day black bus boycott at Montgomery, thirty miles up the road, starting December 5, 1955
- President Eisenhower's use of troops to enforce the integration of Central High School in Little Rock, Arkansas, in 1957
- Turmoil during desegregation of the University of Georgia, January 10, 1961
- Riots at the University of Mississippi, quelled by federalized National Guard and regular army troops on September 30, 1962
- Mass demonstrations in Birmingham, Alabama, in April and May 1963, ending in a far-reaching civil liberties agreement negotiated by business and civic leaders
- Alabama's own earlier skirmish with an integration attempt that backfired on the black students.

All of these, and more, provided clues for how the university should develop its strategy. Staff members studied news accounts and court decisions. The unknown factor was the governor, George Corley Wallace. The feisty and stubborn ex-boxing champion and county judge was politically strong, and his segregation stand was popular. It appeared he could close the university with a snap of the fingers.

But Wallace was a paradox. On the one hand, he stood foursquare for segregation; on the other, he seemed to have a spark of understanding for the blacks' plight in his state. I had an interview with the governor at the height of the Alabama trouble. He appeared almost plaintive in his desire that his sentiments be understood. "I don't hate them," he said of Alabama blacks. "We have lived together in Alabama all my life. I can work with them, and they can work with me."

The showdown came in the late spring of 1963 when it was decided by federal courts that two black students would be registered at the University of Alabama for the summer term. National and international news teams who would report this event began checking in to Tuscaloosa around June 1. Immediately, the signs were obvious that this place was different from the others—advance measures had been taken. The first evidence was that the town showed no signs of tension.

With its wealth of information about the experience of others, the University of Alabama had developed a well-planned strategy. The university could not control what the governor would do; it could, and would, control what the institution and the public did. The key word was order.

"My most vivid recollection is how quiet the campus was," recalled J. Jefferson Bennett, an associate professor who later became president of the university. "They blocked all the traffic, and it was beautifully quiet." Bennett, who served as an aide to University President Frank Rose in 1963, remembered that all soft drink machines on the campus had their glass bottles exchanged for paper cups, and "there wasn't a stick of wood on the campus, or anything else to throw."

Buford Boone, editor of the *Tuscaloosa News*, welcomed several hundred reporters to a fully equipped newsroom in downtown Tuscaloosa. His paper had recently moved into a new plant, and the old one was temporarily vacant. In the next days this was the place for daily briefings, to learn what was happening and, primarily, to be accredited as working press.

We were also given the rules of the university right from the start:

- Anyone on the campus without acceptable identification would be ordered to leave or be arrested.
- Students taking part in demonstrations would be disciplined or sent home.
- News professionals would have free passage on the campus, so long as they were reporting news, and not making news.
- The university would cooperate with the press by providing a regular flow of information and interview contacts.

On June 6, 1963, Federal Judge Seybourne H. Lynne, a personal friend of the governor, ordered Wallace not to interfere with the integration of the university. In an unusually personal and deeply felt statement, Lynne's order included these words:

"In the final analysis, the concept of law and order, the very concept of a republican form of government, embraces the notion that when the judicial process of a state or federal court, acting within the sphere of its competence, has been exhausted and has resulted in a final judgment, all persons affected thereby are obliged to obey it.

"May it be forgiven if this court makes use of the personal pronoun for the first time in a written opinion. I love the people of Alabama. I know that many of both races are troubled and, like Jonah of old, are 'angry even unto death' as the result of distortion of affairs within this state, practiced in the name of sensationalism.

"My prayer is that all of our people, in keeping with our finest traditions, will join in the resolution that law and order will be maintained."

I needed a way to get my Alabama story to UPI. Across the road from the fenced campus was a house. I knew there would be a phone, and probably an occupant curious about what was happening. I knocked on the door and met a woman who was in the retail clothing business. I explained my plight, and she happily invited me to use her phone and work space.

Other UPI reporters, already on campus, had obtained, from where I knew not, nor from whom, a very nice couple of military talk boxes—one for inside, one for outside. We were in business: from campus to house, from house to UPI in Atlanta. And that's the way the Alabama story was covered. At some point in the long morning our hostess left her work, came over to my table and said, just like a mother: "I don't know just what you're doing, but surely you need to go to the bathroom." I took a break.

The governor moved units of the 31st (Dixie) Division of the Alabama National Guard and more than eight hundred state troopers commanded by Colonel Albert J. Lingo, as well as game wardens, into Tuscaloosa. They closed off the campus to the unauthorized, and the governor advised President Kennedy that he was taking the step to preserve peace, and that alone.

Wallace told the president "my presence guarantees peace." Kennedy had asked him to stay away from the scene. Throughout the Tuscaloosa confrontation, Wallace kept the White House informed of his moves; he briefed his staff repeatedly on the urgency of preserving order. He insisted he was raising constitutional, not racial, issues.

Alabama Governor George Wallace talks with reporters during an appearance at WAPI-TV in Birmingham in 1963. Photo: © Joseph M. Chapman

As state and federal authorities arrived on the campus, they toured the layout together to identify buildings and spots where the coming action would occur. Wallace, warned in advance that any violence would be put down, was advised that the army had moved twenty-five hundred troops into Fort McClellan at Anniston, 120 miles to the east. In this confrontation, federal and state forces worked well together.

On Tuesday, June 11, Vivian Malone and James A. Hood, twenty-year-old black applicants, came to the Tuscaloosa campus, accompanied by federal agents and Deputy U.S. Attorney General Nicholas deB. Katzenbach, veteran of the Mississippi confrontation. The Alabama governor arrived the same day. He told reporters, "Don't get in any trouble. Enjoy your stay in Alabama."

The black students were greeted with courtesy, but also with curiosity, by the white students. While the blacks waited in nearby dormitory rooms, Katzenbach went to Foster Auditorium, the registration site. There he was met by Governor Wallace, grim faced and determined to run this act to the finish. As he had promised, the governor planted himself in the doorway to prevent the final event that would topple segregation at the state university.

"From the outset, Governor," Katzenbach told Wallace, "all of us have known that the final chapter of this history will be the admission of these students." He seemed to know already that Wallace was putting on a show.

Katzenbach read to Wallace in a strained voice an order from the president:

"I, John F. Kennedy, president of the United States of America, under and by virtue of the authority vested in me by the Constitution and statutes of the United States . . . do command the governor of the state of Alabama and all other persons engaged or who may engage in unlawful obstructions of justice, assemblies, combinations, conspiracies or domestic violence in that state to cease and desist therefrom."

Katzenbach asked Wallace to accept the order and admit the black students. Four times he asked, and four times Wallace refused. Once, Wallace raised his hand as Katzenbach was talking and said: "Don't make a speech."

Katzenbach: "Governor, I am not interested in a show. I am interested in the orders of these courts being enforced."

Wallace: "I have a statement. The unwelcome, unwanted, unwarranted, and forceful intrusion upon the campus of the University of Alabama today of the might of the central government offers frightful example of the oppression of the rights, privilege and sovereignty of this state by officers of the federal government.

"This intrusion results solely from force, or threat of force, undignified by any reasonable application of the principle of law, reason, and justice. While some few may applaud these acts, millions of Americans will gaze in sorrow . . . As the governor of the state of Alabama, I do hereby denounce and forbid this illegal and unwarranted action by the central government."

Katzenbach responded: "I take it from that statement that you are going to stand in the door, and that you are not going to carry out the orders of the courts, and that you are going to resist our doing so. Is that correct?"

Wallace replied that "I stand according to my statement."

Katzenbach left quietly, this time without the jeers he had encountered in the past during similar arguments in other places. Although the Alabama campus was tense, by now order still ruled. Completely. Wallace retired to a room in Foster Auditorium to await developments, knowing they would come soon. Both sides were only playing out a scenario, and they knew it.

Wallace's press officer, Bill Jones, passed the word to the media: "He never said he will oppose the armed might of the federal government."

Vivian Malone and James Hood were brought from their dorms to the scene in a three-car convoy. They sat with two federal marshals. The cars were parked fifty feet from Foster Auditorium. The black students rolled down the car windows and strained to hear every word of the exchange. Two National Guard helicopters clattered overhead.

U.S. Attorney Macon Weaver and two other federal officials stepped from the lead car and went to the door of the auditorium. As they approached, Wallace came forward. He was surrounded by state troopers. He held up his hand, palm outward, to stop Weaver at the door.

Weaver: "I have here President Kennedy's proclamation. I have come to ask you for unequivocal assurance that you or anyone under your control will not bar these students."

Wallace: "No comment."

Again the federal government exercised extreme patience. Weaver allowed the governor to read his final statement, five pages long.

The president's proclamation and its formal delivery to the governor were the final steps before Kennedy could federalize the Alabama National Guard, removing it temporarily from command of the governor.

Wallace had brought eight hundred helmeted state police with him for this new major collision in the South between state and federal authority. Most of the troopers were clustered around a mobile radio; they got the first word that President Kennedy had formally put the National Guard under his command.

Oddly, state officials were jubilant. It had been their aim to force President Kennedy to take this drastic step. Jones, the press agent, came from a meeting with Wallace and told reporters, "Well, boys, we won Round One."

About this time, the president delivered a nationwide broadcast asking Americans to examine their consciences concerning the racial issue and the situation in Alabama as it was reaching a climax at that moment. Remember, the president's statement was delivered in 1963, one year before public segregation barriers were struck down by new laws.

This is what the president said to the nation: "The Negro baby born in America today, regardless of the section or the state in which he is born, has about one-half the chance of completing high school as a white baby born in the same place on the same day; one-third the chance of completing college; one-third the chance of becoming a professional man; twice as much chance of becoming unemployed; one-seventh as much chance of earning $10,000 a year; a life expectancy which is seven years shorter and the prospects of earning only half as much in his lifetime.

"This is not a sectional issue. Difficulties over segregation and discrimination exist in every city; in every state of the union, producing in many cities a rising tide of discontent that threatens the public safety. Nor is this a partisan issue. This is not even a legal or legislative issue. We are confronted primarily with a moral issue.

"If an American, because his skin is dark, cannot eat lunch in a restaurant open to the public; if he cannot send his children to the best public school available; if he cannot vote for the public officials who represent him; if in short he cannot enjoy the full and free life which all of us want, then who among us would be content to have the color of his skin changed and stand in his place?

"Who among us would then be content with the counsels of patience and delay? One hundred years of delay have passed since President Lincoln freed the slaves; yet, their heirs, their grandsons, are not fully free. And this nation, for all its hopes and all its boasts, will not be fully free until all its citizens are free . . .

"We have a right to expect that the Negro community will be responsible, a right to expect the law will be fair, that the Constitution will be color blind . . ." so spoke the president.

The army arrived at 1:50 p.m. under Brigadier General Henry Graham, commander of the Alabama National Guard, a native Alabamian, and a friend of Wallace. His troops were in battle dress with fixed bayonets.

Graham walked up to Governor Wallace and told him gravely that "it is my sad duty" to order him to step aside and permit the federal orders to take effect.

"I know this is a bitter pill for you to swallow," the governor responded to Graham. "We shall now return to Montgomery to continue this constitutional fight."

The governor's final remark before leaving the stage was, "I can't fight bayonets with my bare hands"; whereupon he walked to his waiting car.

Three minutes later, Hood stepped into the Alabama auditorium with officials and registered. Miss Malone followed in about a minute. They lunched at the student cafeteria with other students, all white. The state troopers left; the National Guard secured the campus; the University of Alabama was integrated. No casualties; no force; just words.

On May 30, 1965, Vivian Malone became the first black graduate of the university. In 1973, Governor Wallace went out on the Alabama football field and crowned the university's first black homecoming queen. By 1983 10 percent of the student body, about 1,300 students, were black. The late great Paul (Bear) Bryant coached some of his finest football teams with black players.

On May 15, 1972, while he was campaigning for president of the United States on a third party ticket, George Corley Wallace was shot by a white man in a crowd at Baltimore, Maryland. Paralyzed from the waist down and confined to a wheelchair, Wallace's spirit and zest for politics never flickered.

In an interview with UPI's Leon Daniel in 1980, Wallace said his views on race had changed. "Segregation is gone," he said. "It should be gone. I was raised in an atmosphere of segregation. I believed in it. I believed it was in the interest of both races." In another interview with Daniel in 1984, Wallace said race relations had improved since the 1960s. "I'm very proud of the progress we have made in our state," he said.

On January 17, 1983, Wallace was sworn in to his fourth term as governor, helped this time by the votes of blacks who were kept from registering to vote twenty years before. He appointed blacks to two of the highest state administrative positions, and personally sponsored four black legislators for committee chairmanships.

Standing before a huge crowd of supporters, including a number of blacks, Wallace concentrated on help for the poor of all races in his inauguration address.

"A nation that forgets its poor loses its soul," he said. "We are not here to deny the mistakes of the past . . . We have come to renew our faith in the future . . . a government guided by a humble man's sense of duty and mercy and justice."

One might be led to believe that finally this man Wallace had reformed on race, had seen the light, and really was penitent about his long career that bore in the opinions of many the label of racist. But George Wallace was, and would be through life, the consummate politician; part give; part take; part philosophy of "If you can't lick 'em, join 'em." He was quite a showman.

With the fury of those days gone, I am willing to give George Wallace the benefit of the doubt, while vividly remembering one of my own experiences with this perplexing politician. We were together on a national television panel at the climax of a major event along the civil rights trail. Soon after the cameras were rolling, the governor opened a file folder and began reciting alleged, and some actual, mistakes by the news media. It was one of his sly ways of diverting attention from the real story and his responsibility in it.

At the end of the program, I was furious and confronted Wallace about his antics. With a cat-swallowing-a-mouse grin on his face, he said: "I didn't mean any harm. I didn't think a big-shot newsman would mind a little old country boy having some fun."

Rosa Parks sits in the front of a bus in Montgomery, Alabama, after the Supreme Court ruled on December 21, 1956, that segregation is illegal on the city bus system. When Parks was arrested on December 1, 1955, for refusing to give up her seat in the front of a bus in Montgomery, it set off a successful boycott of the city buses. The man sitting behind Parks is Nicholas C. Chriss, a reporter for United Press International out of Atlanta. Photo: © Bettmann-Corbis

CHAPTER 6

1955-1964–Rosa Parks and Her Famous Bus Ride

"The term Satyagraha was coined by me . . . Its root meaning is 'holding on to truth' . . . I discovered in the earliest stages that pursuit of truth did not permit violence being inflicted on one's opponent, but that he must be weaned from error by patience and sympathy. For what appears truth to the one may appear to be error to the other."

—Mohandas Gandhi

Accident, anger, pride, stubbornness, just being caught up in the fervor of a big crowd going somewhere—many were the reasons why people, black and white, were propelled onto one side or the other of the civil rights struggles of the mid-twentieth century.

Martin Luther King, Jr., was one of those propelled. His admirers believed this was not accident, but destiny. He saw himself as an obstacle remover, a Joshua with a small unarmed band surrounding a powerful enemy. In this case segregation was the enemy, and, as the old song goes, "The walls came tumbling down."

King's part in the drama began in 1955 in the Dexter Avenue Baptist Church in Montgomery, an unpretentious two-story building about five hundred yards down the hill from the Alabama state capitol. A church auditorium was on the main floor, a Sunday school room in the basement.

Introducing the "Mother of Civil Rights"

On December 1, a black woman was arrested in Montgomery for refusing a bus driver's order to move out of the section reserved for whites. Soon after the arrest, I met King for the first time there in the Sunday school department. It had been eighteen months since the Supreme Court ruled that the doctrine of separate-but-equal was no longer valid in public education.

These had been months of ever-so-grudging compliance with the new decision, and also months of determined resistance to the mandate. Blacks, with the law finally on their side—at least as it applied to education—were finding that the toughest battles were still ahead. In Montgomery, there were rising expectations among blacks and stonewall unyielding among most whites. King was in the midst of this ferment—as a minister, as counselor to blacks, and as a black man himself.

As I walked down the center aisle of the Sunday school room, King sat working alone at a small table. He looked up as I approached and said, "Good morning. Welcome." He was dressed in a blue work shirt and denims. He was just twenty-six and named for the great German Protestant reformer, Martin Luther (changed from Michael Luther when the boy was five by "Daddy" King who liked it so much he changed his own as well). I noted that King was short and husky, that his skin was olive-toned, that his face was round, and that he had a resonant, baritone voice. I would see and hear him many times in the days and nights ahead.

Once he compared himself to Socrates as one of the "creative gadflies of society." He had a way of reducing complex issues to terms that anyone could understand. When there was widespread discontent among blacks about their struggle for equality of employment, King urged young people to prepare themselves for jobs, reminding them that "it does no good to be able to eat at a lunch counter if you can't afford to buy a hamburger."

There were those who maintained that full civil rights would have come to the black people anyway, regardless of King and his followers. His detractors reasoned that the time was ripe for the transition; that the South was ready for acceptance of a new way; that no one objected to integration "when the niggers are ready for it." If the outside agitators like "Nigger King" would stay away, it would be handled in good time—that's what was said. But the tide of rising expectations could not be held back to "get ready." The black chant in rally after rally was: "Freedom is now."

Montgomery, capital of the state of Alabama and earlier capital of the Confederacy, was a quiet town of Southern grace and charm in the 1950s. In the spring, flowers and shrubs burst into a kaleidoscope of breathtaking beauty, but only nature was not segregated in Montgomery. It was a setting that generations of white settlers had enjoyed and loved—and that blacks had accepted because it was their only option.

Until desegregation pressures heightened in the mid-1950s, there was general racial peace in Montgomery, so long as blacks "knew their place." The town was somewhat of a safe harbor for blacks from the nearby rural countryside. I have heard blacks in trouble say if they could only get to Montgomery they felt safe. There were pockets of blacks all over Montgomery, but it was not like many Southern communities where blacks lived only in "Nigger Town."

King's church occupied choice property on Dexter Avenue, that broad thoroughfare along which Jefferson Davis had ridden to his inauguration as president of the Confederate States of America less than a century earlier. It was when "outsiders stirred up our good niggers," as I heard it so often expressed, that race relations in Montgomery suffered. Some whites with whom I talked were sincerely saddened at the turn of events. They seemed so sure that life should go on unchanged.

Although he always claimed to be primarily a minister, it was not the pulpit that propelled King into world prominence, but the Montgomery bus system. Because of a few buses, his name became a byword in Asia, Africa, South America, and Europe, as well as in the United States.

The bus system of Montgomery obtained a major portion of its revenue from black riders in a city where blacks and whites were very nearly equal in the population. The buses were racially segregated in a particular way, by use of rules that went much further than city ordinance and state statute.

It was a general practice at all times that the first ten rows of seats in the front of a bus were reserved for white passengers. In addition, there were signs labeled "white" and "colored" that could be fitted above the windows. As the number of white riders increased, the operator moved the window signs toward the rear, providing more seats for whites, fewer for blacks. This often meant that blacks were required to leave seats and stand packed into the rear of buses as the signs were shifted.

The buses' "nigger signs"—as they were called—caused bitterness which could be likened to a sore that festered and erupted, scabbed over and festered again. Black leaders, using the meager communications they had with whites of Montgomery, tried to ease that point of racial tension by gaining agreement to remove the signs. They were unsuccessful. In time, they formed the Montgomery Improvement Association to give themselves an organized voice. King became its president.

He preached on at the Dexter Avenue Baptist Church, but the tone of his sermons changed. From the pulpit, he began speaking of freedom for the black people. He challenged them to prepare for a great adventure. And in the adventuring, he urged them to dedicate their lives to a philosophy of non-violence. He said it was to be a new era for their race.

King preached in those days against a backdrop of significant events in the area of race relations. Wherever a large segment of non-whites was concentrated in the nation, or in the world for that matter, something new was stirring among them.

The cry of "Uhuru!" (Freedom!) that rang out around the globe in the 1950s and 1960s came from an ocean away, in Africa. But it was the same voice that was heard in Montgomery, Alabama. It was not a political phenomenon, although it made use of politics. It was a bold affirmation that humankind, collective and individual, is created to be free and not exploited. It was an awareness hinted at in the Magna Carter in England and expanded in the Declaration of Independence and the Constitution in the United States of America.

There was to be much trial and error in the years ahead: mistakes, advance, and retreat, destruction, death—and growth for mankind, dark and light. I believe I realized even then in the infancy of this new civil rights movement that the echo of freedom will be heard around the world in one form or another until it is completely accepted by all, and thoroughly satisfying for those who seek it.

On the morning of December 1, 1955, these voices of freedom stirred and were heard in the Southern city of Montgomery, Alabama. On that morning, Rosa Parks, who rode twice daily to and from her job as a domestic servant, stepped onto a bus and sat down—some recall it was in a seat reserved for whites; others, including Dr. King, maintained the black woman was actually sitting in an unreserved section. At any rate, she refused to move when the startled driver ordered her to sit further back in the bus. He stopped the bus at the next corner and called a policeman.

Mrs. Parks was arrested and removed from the bus. At police headquarters she was booked and gave her name. The charge against her was disturbing the peace. She was tried and convicted. Her police court fine was fourteen dollars, increased to $41.35 when her conviction was upheld in Montgomery circuit court. The court action became insignificant after that, for there is no record that she ever paid a fine or spent time in jail.

At Dexter Avenue Baptist Church, where Mrs. Parks was a member, young Dr. King made his move. He called on the blacks of Montgomery to begin a nonviolent protest for Rosa Parks and against bus segregation. He asked them to stop riding buses until the segregation signs came down, and they responded to the call enthusiastically. Almost overnight, King became the leader in the nonviolent movement against racial discrimination in the United States.

Although he moved into an arena where these goals had been sought for many years by the National Association for the Advancement of Colored People, the National Urban League, the Brotherhood of Sleeping Car Porters—and others—his kind of leadership and method of operating were very different. King was more urgent, more daring, and more assertive for the right of racial equality.

Before the Montgomery bus boycott was finished, King knew that he had a national audience—and he used it expertly and repeatedly.

King told a white audience: "We will match your capacity to inflict suffering with our capacity to endure suffering. We will meet your physical force with soul force. We will not hate you, but we cannot in all good conscience obey your unjust laws. We will soon wear you down by our capacity to suffer, and in winning our freedom, we will so appeal to your heart and conscience that we will win you in the process."

King spoke eloquently when he was with a business or political assembly, but his approach was different with the poor and deprived on the civil rights trail. "So, listen to me, Children," he said. "Put on your marching shoes. Don't you get weary. Though the path ahead may be dark and dreary, we are walking for freedom, Children." He was convinced that "history has thrust me into this position, and it would be both immoral and a sign of ingratitude if I did not face my moral responsibility to do what I can in this struggle."

He came into view like a comet, flashed across the horizon, and was gone. King died of an assassin's bullet only twelve years after the day I first met him in Montgomery. Let us not get ahead of the story; in that brief span, he played out a role that cannot be touched for its social significance. That day, standing at his card table office in Montgomery, King was just a young black preacher with a certain shyness still about him; but he already had a stubborn tilt to his chubby jaw. Beyond the city limits of Montgomery, except for family, lifetime friends, and school associates, it seemed young King was almost unknown. That changed very swiftly.

For thousands of leaderless blacks, this was high drama to have such a leader. Here was one who had the enthusiasm and foolhardiness of youth, one who had charisma that could silence a roaring crowd or send frightened children into the streets marching. Whatever brought him to the Dexter Avenue Baptist Church, for the purpose of his mission King arrived at the right place at the right time.

In speech after speech to the bus boycotters, he urged nonviolence, persistence, determination, and courage. And the collection baskets were passed at almost all of those rallies. Early in his campaign, however, King realized that the big money he said was needed for the long-term drive to break segregation must come from outside the South. He went for it.

King delivered one of the more stirring addresses of his short career while the bus boycott was in effect. It was far from Montgomery before the national convention of the National Association for the Advancement of Colored People in San Francisco, California, on June 27, 1956, about midway of the boycott. Roy Wilkins, head of the NAACP, could not always subscribe to the tactics of King's organization, but he loved the young black preacher who always to him was "Martin." Wilkins invited King to talk about Montgomery, and this is what "Martin" had to say:

"The story of Montgomery is the story of fifty thousand Negroes who are tired of injustice and oppression, and who are willing to substitute tired feet for tired souls, and walk, and walk, and walk until the sagging walls of injustice have been finally crushed by the battering rams of historical necessity.

" . . . From the beginning, there has been a basic philosophy under girding the (Montgomery) movement. It is a philosophy of non-violent resistance. It is simply a refusal, in a non-violent sense, to cooperate with the evil of segregation."

He said any attempt to use violence in the Montgomery boycott would be "both impractical and immoral. Violence creates many more problems than it solves. There is a voice crying through the vista of time saying: 'He who lives by the sword shall die by the sword.'"

King denied that "real tension" existed between white and black people in Montgomery, or elsewhere. "The tension at bottom is between justice and injustice." He ended his San Francisco address with words I heard him use so many times in those church meeting campaigns in the South: "We must keep moving. If you can't fly, run; if you can't run, walk; if you can't walk, crawl— but by all means keep moving." And he caught a plane back to Montgomery.

The blacks of Montgomery boycotted the buses for a year. They clustered around makeshift wood burners on street corners, waiting for winter rides to their jobs; otherwise, they walked, walked, walked. White people were certain at first that the blacks could not hold out for long. When they did hold out, for days, then weeks, then months, many white housewives unashamedly began "going after the help."

It became a dramatic story—this silent, peaceful battle of the powerless Negroes against the bus company and the Montgomery segregation policy.

Outside help began to come: money, food, clothing, legal advice. Their case went to court after awhile—again on constitutional grounds—and there they won. The signs came down. The blacks could sit on the buses where they chose. But even in triumph, King noticed in that early stage of his campaign a disturbing factor. He told a friend after the victory: "Negroes can ride where they want to on the buses, but there is more bitterness in the city now than ever before."

His was not an easy leadership. King was maligned, accused, and blasphemed by his detractors—and there were many, black as well as white. He became the object of attacks and vilification; his home was bombed; he was spat upon and kicked, struck, and mobbed; he was stabbed by a black woman in New York City; he was frequently jailed. His wife learned to ignore anonymous telephone calls and burning crosses—symbol of the Ku Klux Klan—on the lawn of the Kings' Atlanta home. Blacks who did not like his style labeled him "Uncle Tom"—a term intended to be derogatory, denoting blacks bowing to white domination. He was to see the day when bitterness would also turn on him, when the yellow smear of raw eggs would spatter against his automobile—eggs hurled not by white opponents, but by blacks he thought were his friends.

The arousal of passions haunted King constantly as he moved from city to city with his nonviolent crusade.

In October of 1960, with a presidential race headed for what was expected to be a photo finish and with civil rights one of the campaign's topmost issues, King was jailed after a sit-in demonstration at Rich's Department Store in Atlanta. Suddenly and without official explanation, the Atlanta charges were dropped on the weekend of October 22. But neighboring DeKalb County quickly asked for custody of King on an old traffic charge.

After a trial on October 27, a probation previously handed to the defendant on the traffic count was revoked, and he was ordered to the Reidsville State Prison to serve a four-month sentence. This prison was hated and feared by blacks.

Just two days later, King was free again on a bond agreed to by DeKalb Judge Oscar Mitchell, who had sentenced him. Mitchell's version of what happened was that he had a request from George Stewart, secretary of the Democratic Committee in Georgia, to come to Stewart's home. There, Stewart put it up to him to have King released. Mitchell agreed there might be a way, but nothing was done that night.

Mitchell said the next morning he had a telephone call from Robert Kennedy, brother of the Democratic presidential candidate, who "asked me if there was any way under the Constitution that I could permit King freedom on bond. I told him there was, and I agreed to the bond."

William B. Hartsfield, who was then mayor of Atlanta and as shrewd a politician and staunch Democrat as lived in the state of Georgia, had an entirely different version. At the time all this was happening to King, U.S. Senator John F. Kennedy and Richard Nixon, the Republican nominee, were locked in a bitter, close race for the presidency. Hartsfield said he realized that the black vote was paramount to Kennedy, the Democrat. Telegrams and other messages were flooding the mayor's office objecting to King's arrest, and Hartsfield recalled, "I suddenly realized the tremendous power of this issue."

The mayor said he asked Atlanta black preachers to come to city hall to negotiate with him about ending sit-in demonstrations sweeping the city. While they were in the meeting, Hartsfield said he and two associates went to the mayor's private office. There they telephoned the Democratic National Committee in Washington and talked with Harris Wofford, who was in charge of the campaign with minority groups. After unsuccessful efforts to reach Kennedy personally, Hartsfield said he told Wofford he was going to announce to the black ministers that Kennedy had intervened to gain King's release from jail.

"This I did," Hartsfield said. "The committee got to Kennedy and he bought it in a flash."

Whichever version of the story was absolutely correct, Senator John Kennedy telephoned King's wife, Coretta, in a dramatic personal expression of sympathy for her husband. Kennedy went on to win the presidential race against Nixon.

Hartsfield was jubilant and stood firm on his story. "I got King out and fixed it so Kennedy got the credit so as to help his campaign," he said. "When I told those preachers that Kennedy was intervening, one of them left the room. He was a top Republican, and I let him use the phone to call his national committee. At the same time, I was on the other phone to the Democrats. Nixon couldn't be reached by his man. Had he been, and had he intervened for King, it could have put the Republicans in the White House."

In the aftermath of this political spectacle, the Atlanta mayor insisted that he had no desire to criticize the DeKalb County court for its swift and tough handling of the King case. "But I have made requests to all news agencies that in their stories they make it clear that this hearing did not take place in Atlanta."

Like King himself, the organization he formed appeared to be a temporary structure, destined to rise to strength and influence for a specific purpose, and then to decline when its primary mission was accomplished. In the accomplishing, it collected millions of dollars and was loved and hated with almost equal fervor.

King's reliance on federal protection was shaky. He had the strong public support of the new president and the attorney general of the United States—John F. Kennedy and his brother, Robert, whom JFK appointed as the nation's top lawyer—but the Federal Bureau of Investigation, the enforcement arm of the attorney general's office, was not always cooperative. J. Edgar Hoover, then director of the FBI, despised King.

In Houston, Texas, in 1969, FBI Agent Robert Nichols testified in federal court that the agency maintained telephone surveillance on King for several years. He explained that the phone tap was done while King was accusing the FBI of assigning Southern instead of non-Southern agents to protect civil rights workers.

The FBI has an acknowledged file of 78,816 pages of material on King, his movement, and his subsequent assassination—interviews, statements, and general activities. In addition, on January 31, 1977, District of Columbia Federal Judge John Lewis Smith, Jr., ordered the FBI to turn over to the National Archives all known copies of tapes, transcripts, and logs of microphone and telephone surveillance of Dr. King and the organization he led. Under the court order, that material will remain under seal until the year 2027.

Regardless of his difficulties with friends as well as enemies, there was no doubt that King was the master architect of the civil rights movement in the 1960s.

From the moment he left his card table headquarters in the Dexter Avenue Baptist Church in Montgomery to the moment he was felled by a bullet on a Memphis motel balcony, King was in command of a strategic force.

King had an inner sense that he had been shoved on stage to direct a certain part of the drama, and he knew that it was crucial to the whole show. All the while, King was haunted by the likelihood that blacks outside his own organization would stir up trouble that would destroy his nonviolent effort. Often he held his people for hours in prayer meetings to prepare them for nonviolence before sending them out to confront the forces of segregation.

Trying to calm those who wanted to take up arms, he told an audience in Gadsden, Alabama: "Some of you have knives; I ask you to put them up. Some of you have arms; I ask you to put them up. Get the weapon of nonviolence, the breastplate of righteousness, the armor of truth, and just keep marching."

King did not win all his campaigns. The first black effort to integrate everything at once occurred in the South Georgia town of Albany in 1962. It failed because the local leadership carefully avoided outright confrontation. The drive dragged on for months, first at the black church, then at the county courthouse. The white city government didn't say "Yes" and didn't say "No" to black demands, and the effort began to lose popular appeal with the demonstrators. At the same time, violence began to develop on the fringes of the crowd.

One drizzly night, several hundred blacks were camped on the broad courthouse lawn at Albany, waiting for an answer to their latest appeal. The hours dragged on past midnight; lights burned in the courthouse, but no one appeared. Reporters, with access to both sides of the confrontation, picked up comments from blacks in the crowd: they were weary; they wanted to quit; but they were afraid to walk back to their church.

Two journalists went to authorities in the courthouse and told them that the demonstrators were ready to give up, but they wanted protection back to their church. The safeguard was quickly granted by an escort of officers. The blacks agreed to disperse quietly; they walked silently to the church. The Albany campaign was over.

One day in Birmingham, King left his motel for a short walk to a church where a full house of young racial demonstrators awaited his orders to march into the streets. He looked searchingly across to where a crowd of about a hundred blacks stood silently, watching developments. I was walking beside King and heard him say reflectively: "You know, I'm not concerned about the people in the church. I believe they will remain nonviolent. I'm not even bothered about the police or the other white people in Birmingham. I'm worried about that crowd across the street."

It was at such times that King was almost overcome by his sense of power over his own people, and lack of it among those who insisted on violence. "The influence I somehow have over people frightens me," he said. I could tell it was a deeply felt physical fear. Not only did he have dedicated adult believers with him but hundreds of young school children. He said "one of the most difficult things I have to deal with is convincing these followers that if our effort is to succeed, they must be nonviolent." King developed his own philosophy of peaceful resistance from studying the world's great philosophers and from the experience of the Mahatma Gandhi of India, who used that method to overthrow British rule of his country. In King's own case, nonviolence often was a very fragile thread.

King was saddened and perplexed when blacks turned against him, and he wondered if one of them, instead of some white segregationist, might assume the role of his assassin. Occasionally, as the campaign advanced, he talked of a premonition of death. "I cannot stop," he said when his lieutenants begged him to stay away from a dangerous situation. "If I must die, I must die, and others must carry on."

The nation was his stage, and he went to the spots where the actors whom he needed for specific results were to be found. He used situations to influence public opinion, to goad a foot-dragging Congress, to change laws, to topple barriers. If it meant death, as it did sometimes to those in his campaign; if it meant jail, which happened more often than not; if it meant a further polarization of opposing forces, in his mind it was all part of what seemed to be the necessary price of gaining equality.

Thus it was that King used long and bitter demonstrations in Birmingham to convince Congress of the need for a Civil Rights Act that would guarantee the rights of all people to the use of public accommodations. Thus it was that a bruising, rain-soaked ordeal in Selma, Alabama, and a subsequent fifty-mile march through rural countryside, were used to press for congressional passage of a new voting rights provision. And thus it was that a campaign was mounted in St. Augustine, Florida, to prod the Congress into passage of a section in the 1964 Civil Rights Act that would end forever the segregation of hotels and motels, public eating places, and recreation.

"The deep rumbling of discontent that we hear today is the thunder of disinherited masses, rising from dungeons of oppression to the bright hills of freedom," he told a rally in Alabama, using words that were sent around the world by the ever-present news media.

"If the people of good will of the white South fail to act now, history will have to record that the greatest evil of this period of social transition was not the vitriolic words and the violent actions of the bad people, but the appalling silence and indifference of good people.

"We will take direct action against injustice without waiting for other agencies to act. We will not obey unjust laws or submit to unjust practices . . . Our aim is a community at peace with itself, and we are ready to suffer when necessary and even risk our lives to become witnesses to the truth as we see it."

There was purpose and strategy in all that Martin Luther King Jr. did. The moves he made, once the civil rights crusade got under way following the Montgomery bus boycott victory, were carefully worked out in closed door meetings with his team.

Not long after the U.S. Supreme Court affirmed a lower court decision that the buses in Montgomery must maintain non-segregated seating, King pulled his ragtag but successful organization off the streets of the Alabama capital city and built it into a structure given the name of the Southern Christian Leadership Conference. Headquarters were established in Atlanta, Georgia, on Auburn Avenue in the heart of a long-thriving black business district.

King was now a long way from that card table office in the basement of a church. The civil rights struggle of the 1960s was in full cry.

Mourners leave church after a funeral for three of the four girls killed in the bombing of the Sixteenth Street Baptist Church in Birmingham, Alabama, in 1963. Photo: © Joseph M. Chapman

CHAPTER 7

1963–Courage v. Dogs and Dynamite in Birmingham

"Why should there not be a patient confidence in the ultimate justice of the people? Is there any better or equal hope in the world?"

President Abraham Lincoln

WASHINGTON, D. C., January 14, 1963—President John F. Kennedy, in his State of the Union address to Congress, only briefly mentioned civil rights, and said the "overshadowing" domestic problem in the United States was the need for a tax cut to stimulate economic growth.

MONTGOMERY, ALA., January 14, 1963—Governor George C. Wallace said in his inaugural address: "Let us rise to the call of freedom-loving blood that is in us, and send our answer to the tyranny that clanks its chains upon the South."

Restraint Despite Bombing

By 1963, civil rights activists, backed by thousands of blacks in the streets, insisted on total integration—not just in education. Those who remembered recent history recognized the battle lines being drawn. Just six years before, Congress had passed the first new civil rights act in eighty-two years. It gave the attorney general the right to seek injunctions against those depriving people of the right to vote. But a key section of that legislation—strongly urged by then President Eisenhower—was defeated. It was a public accommodations section: motels, hotels, eating places, swimming pools. Here was an omen of the difficulties ahead, and blacks began stepping up their fight against any discrimination.

Some of the most dramatic and effective campaigns of the civil rights thrust in the mid-twentieth century began spontaneously—small sparks that

71

lit big fires. One chilly day in 1960, four black students at State Teachers College in Greensboro, North Carolina, sat in a dormitory room wondering what they could do for the new civil rights movement. On the spur of the moment, one of them recalled later, they decided to go to downtown Greensboro and try to get lunch at the Woolworth Five-and-Ten at 132 South Elm.

That one impulsive act sent shock waves through the segregated store's management, and throughout the Land of Segregation. Within a year of the incident, the national sit-in movement was launched, and eating barriers began to topple—not always without violence. Many stores closed eating facilities; others ripped out counter stools, and customers ate standing up—which was a new experience for white shoppers. One innovative establishment in Atlanta, Georgia, conducted an informal survey to determine the fast-food preference of blacks who came to the store and opened a second fast-food grill in the basement featuring those food items. It was soon frequented by blacks, leaving the spaces upstairs for whites—some of whom began joining blacks in the basement because the food was so good.

Also in Atlanta, a fairly high-class barbecue chicken restaurant called The Pickrick—owned by one Lester Maddox—became the scene of a daily lunchtime confrontation between Maddox, who proclaimed that his political beliefs barred him from serving blacks, and a group of young black activists. They came punctually each noon for lunch.

To the cheers of his white patrons, who had front table seats at the restaurant's plate glass windows, the balding Maddox would storm out of the place to challenge the "intruders" in the parking lot. Often, he came swinging a small wooden bat and yelling—but not obscenities, for he was a professed religious man. The bats became popular souvenirs with patrons, so the enterprising Maddox, ever mindful of a way to make a buck, began stocking them for sale as "Pickrick Axe Handles." I had many a good barbecue lunch there while reporting on the action, paying the bill at a cash register on which perched a huge black bird that squawked: "Come again; come again!"

Lester Maddox parlayed his segregation demonstration into one of the oddest political triumphs in Georgia or American history: without previous political activity or experience, he was elected to a term as governor, largely on the basis of his segregation activity.

The fear that Southern blacks, if they ever got the chance, would vote themselves into public office, was a very real apprehension and became a reality in the mid-twentieth century for the first time since the Reconstruction period after the Civil War. In the Georgia legislature seven black members, all from predominantly black districts, were seated. There were rumblings, but no open opposition. Then came No. 8, a twenty-five-year-old anti-Vietnam War activist named Julian Bond. I well remember that night of January 10, 1966, in a scene part serious and part theatrical, when young Bond came into the House chamber for a special hearing to determine if he should be sworn in.

Bond had studied philosophy under Martin Luther King, Jr., at Morehouse College, a black institution in Atlanta, and when he decided to enter politics, his first campaign was run from donated upstairs space in a black restaurant. Twice, after being elected, Bond was denied his seat.

Boyish but self-assured, Bond sat quietly listening as other blacks were sworn in routinely. But his was no routine case. He was accused of disloyalty to the country and thus unfit to serve. Bond was no stranger to the Georgia legislature. A few years before, he was ejected for refusing to sit in the segregated section of the House gallery. Now it was his turn to speak.

Stepping to the well of the House before a full complement of legislators and a packed gallery, Bond defended his right to serve, eloquently but without passion claiming that this right had nothing to do with whether others supported his beliefs. He said it was his privilege as a citizen to oppose what he considered an unjust war. He refused to repudiate a statement condemning the Vietnam conflict. A white legislator next to me muttered: "Listen to that nigger. He talks as good as we do."

The speech did Bond no good. He received only twelve favorable votes. The U.S. Supreme Court finally ruled on December 5, 1966, that Bond's rights had been violated and ordered that he be seated.

Meanwhile Southern governors talked seriously of "interposing" the eminent domain of a state's rights as a means of "nullifying" federal rulings on civil rights. Violence spread; vigilantes were everywhere, linked together by short wave radio; fear was rampant. I had a telephone call late one night from a colleague in the New York office of UPI, an enlightened fellow who was unflappable most of the time. He said he had planned to drive with his family to New Orleans on vacation and wondered if it would be safe to go through Alabama and Mississippi with New York license plates on his car. It was that bad.

On February 28, 1963, the president sent to Congress civil rights requests again largely dealing only with voting rights. He called for legislation to:

(1) Authorize appointment of temporary voting referees to register blacks in counties where voting rights suits had been filed, and where fewer than 15 percent of voting-age blacks were registered;

(2) Expedite resolution of civil rights suits in federal courts;
(3) Establish a sixth-grade education as a presumption of literacy;
(4) Provide federal, technical, and financial assistance to school districts that were in the process of desegregating;
(5) Extend the Civil Rights Commission for four more years and designate it as a national clearinghouse for civil rights.

Any other time, it might have been an acceptable package, but not now; not in 1963. The proposed legislation was criticized by liberal Democrats and Republicans as being too weak for the times. New York Governor Nelson Rockefeller, a Republican, charged that President Kennedy had "abdicated virtually all leadership toward achieving necessary civil rights legislation" and had settled for "administrative actions of high publicity value."

The oratory had hardly stopped resounding in the halls of Congress before an echo came back from the streets of Birmingham, Alabama. On April 3 mass demonstrations for a strong civil rights law, including a section to open the doors of public places to everyone, began in Birmingham and spread rapidly through the South and beyond.

Even in those frenzied times, however, some cities were coming to terms with the civil rights issue. On May 19, 1963, the Board of Aldermen of Louisville, Kentucky, voted 9-3 to outlaw discrimination in public business places. Thus, Louisville won the distinction of being the first Southern city to adopt its own open public accommodations act.

In Spartanburg, South Carolina, the mayor and city council sat down with the black leadership without waiting for racial groups to carry out a plan to mount demonstrations. The meeting led to peaceful desegregation without fanfare, and almost without publicity.

As the biracial meeting ended, DeQuincy Newman, the state representative of the National Association for the Advancement of Colored People, was asked if he had anything further to say. "Yes," he replied. "We would consider it an act of good faith if a start could be made toward desegregation of a few public accommodations."

One member of the city council, owner of a chain of drug stores, spoke: "The lunch counters of my drug stores will be desegregated this afternoon. Would you consider that an act of good faith?"

"Yes, indeed I would," Newman answered.

When the federal courts ordered Alabama public schools desegregated, some areas reluctantly but peacefully complied—but not Birmingham. Four frightened black pupils were brought to West End High School in a middle-class white residential neighborhood. For three days they were subjected to isolation inside the building and to the jeers of a throng of white students who were outside, boycotting classes.

Communications was a problem for news crews covering the turbulent event. I visited a home across the street from the school and made a deal to rent a phone for one day at five dollars. It worked so well that I went back to pay for another day's use. "Sorry," said the lady, "today it will be 100 dollars." I turned down the offer and went looking for another communications source.

In those days the telephone company worked closely with the wire services because of the huge revenue involved, so I thought to ask a favor. I wanted the local phone company to install a temporary phone outlet on a specific telephone pole near the school. No problem, I was told. Later on, this could never happen, but it did then, and that was the important thing. I had the phone in operation in one hour.

UPI reporter Al Kuettner, using a special telephone on a pole near the West End High School campus, is surrounded by Confederate flag-waving students protesting racial integration of the school in September 1963. Photo: United Press International

The private phone was kept in the trunk of my car and plugged in to the outlet on the pole when I needed to call my office in Atlanta. This worked well for awhile until those boisterous students began gathering around to hear what was being dictated. They did not like what they heard. Bright youngsters that they were, they soon figured they could easily disconnect the circuit by unplugging the phone. This they did, not once but many times.

Finally in frustration I out-yelled the crowd. "OK, you guys," I shouted. "If you don't like the way I do it, talk yourself." They lined up to give their reactions, which were dutifully taken down by a staff member in Atlanta. We had a good story, and my phone was not bothered again.

The West End story ended with perhaps some sore throats from screaming, but no one was hurt, and integration was a fact in the steel city.

The U.S. Department of Justice sent the president a report showing that between May 22 and June 15 of 1963, some 143 cities had taken steps to remove racial barriers. All were in the Deep South, plus Maryland, West Virginia, Kentucky, and Oklahoma. And in Oxford, Mississippi, James Meredith graduated with a degree in political science from the University of

Al Kuettner interviews three black girls integrating Jones Valley High School near the western edge of Birmingham, Alabama, in 1963. Kuettner was an eyewitness to many key events of the civil rights movement, covering it from the 1950s into the 1960s. Photo: © Joseph M. Chapman

Mississippi. It was just fifteen months after his enrollment as the first black student to attend the university.

Birmingham in the early 1960s was the steel capital of the South, home of the Tennessee Coal and Iron Co., Southern outreach of U.S. Steel. Mills were in the valley between two ranges of mountains—one supplying coal, the other iron ore, to the glowing furnaces.

In the blue collar world of Birmingham, life was tough for workers in the mills and mines. The city's population was 30 percent black. There had been vicious flare ups between whites and blacks, but nothing that could not be controlled by the authorities.

The police commissioner of Birmingham was Eugene Connor. He was known as "Bull," an apt title to go with his roar and bellicosity. Although he was sometimes an embarrassment to the people who thought of community image, they accepted him because he maintained law and order, and strict obedience to the city's segregation rules. Schools, public restrooms, eating facilities, churches—all were segregated.

Birmingham in 1963 was labeled the most segregated city in the South. Even paths and footbridges across streams in the city zoo were divided down the middle by handrails containing signs to indicate which side was for blacks and which for whites.

At the height of the Birmingham racial troubles of the 1960s blind Negro singer Al Hibbler said that Birmingham police would not arrest him with other demonstrators. He complained, "That is segregation at its highest level."

Sixteen blocks from downtown Birmingham was the office of an extraordinary black man, A.G. Gaston. The office had a desk eight feet long, tailored draperies at the windows, private bath, and ivory statuary which he had collected on one of his several trips to Africa. On the wall opposite his desk, where he could always see it, was a painting of two blacks in front of a cabin, guiding an ox that pulled a farm wagon. The painting was his reminder that he had risen from a thirty-cents-an-hour laborer to become a multi-million dollar insurance and real estate executive. Gaston believed that blacks could make it on their own, if they tried.

In Washington, D.C., with prodding from civil rights organizations, Congress was moving toward consideration of a new civil rights act. In April, Martin Luther King, Jr., moved his Southern Christian Leadership Conference forces into Birmingham to demonstrate to Congress and the White House what the fuss was all about. His move was against the wishes of most local blacks, including A.G. Gaston. But for King, it was the perfect place to show the lack of racial equality, and the need for a new Civil Rights Act.

King's chief lieutenants in the developing campaign were the Reverend Fred Shuttlesworth and the Reverend Ralph David Abernathy. Both were leaders in the Southern Christian Leadership Conference that had been formed with people from inside and outside communities targeted for civil rights campaigns. They were labeled outsiders. Even at the height of the campaign in the steel city, fewer than fifty Birmingham blacks were in the lead of the protest. Not more than two thousand of the area's three hundred thousand blacks ever turned out for major rallies or demonstrations. Shuttlesworth, who was a Cincinnati, Ohio, clergyman, headed the local civil rights group in Birmingham, known as the Alabama Christian Movement for Human Rights. Abernathy, an Atlanta, Georgia, minister, was King's chief assistant.

King and his organization established headquarters in a motel for blacks, owned by Gaston. In keeping with Gaston's philosophy that black businesses must be the best, his motel compared favorably to many on the white side of town. Two blocks from the motel, in the Sixteenth Street Baptist Church, the King organization held nightly rallies. The immediate target was downtown stores that operated restaurants, tea rooms and snack bars. Day after day,

Leaders of the civil rights movement in 1963 increasingly involved children in learning about and helping spread the message. Photo: © Joseph M. Chapman

black pickets and other demonstrators were sent to the target businesses, and as regularly they were hauled off to jail.

One of King's primary strategies was filling the jails with nonviolent demonstrators. He often said that was the only effective way of laying the plight and purpose of black people before the court of public opinion. When the arrests of adults failed to win victory in Birmingham, another nearby source of crowds for the jails was available: hundreds of black children from the schools. They came in waves to workshop sessions at the church, and in waves marched out to the waiting police vehicles. Some of these children, drawn into the activity by the excitement, were as young as ten years of age. Older black youth were recruited. I heard more than one adult say to them, "You're not learning anything in school anyway."

As they were taken to jail, the children clasped the patrol car bars with small fingers and sang shrilly, "Freedom! Freedom!" I asked one of them what he was after, and that's what he told me. The jail finally became overtaxed, and the overflow of more than twenty-two hundred arrested went to the state fairgrounds for incarceration. The jail kitchen crew had an impossible task, requiring as much as four hours to serve so simple a meal as breakfast, consisting of grits, gravy, bacon, and applesauce.

King, himself, was among those jailed, and, true to form, he spent his time there pushing the civil rights movement. In a letter that became briefly famous, King wrote from the jail that "injustice anywhere is a threat to justice everywhere." It became one of the rallying cries of his demonstrators.

Because he was denied writing material in jail, he wrote on toilet paper and smuggled his message out to the news media, answering white ministers of Birmingham who had condemned his tactics. He reminded them—and the world—that "we have waited for more than 340 years for our Constitutional and God-given rights . . . I guess it is easy for those who have never felt the stinging darts of segregation to say 'wait.'

" . . . When you are humiliated day in and day out by nagging signs reading 'white' and 'colored;' when your first name becomes 'nigger' and your middle name becomes 'boy' (however old you are) and when your last name becomes 'John;' and when your wife and mother are never given the respected title 'Mrs.' . . . when you are forever fighting a degenerating sense of 'nobodyness'—then you will understand why we find it difficult to wait.

" . . . Before the Pilgrims landed at Plymouth, we were here. Before the pen of Jefferson etched across the pages of history the majestic words of the Declaration of Independence, we were here. For more than two centuries, our foreparents labored in this country without wages; they made cotton king, and they built the homes of their masters in the midst of brutal injustice and shameful humiliation—and yet out of a bottomless vitality, they continued to thrive and develop. If the inexpressible cruelties of slavery could not stop us, the opposition we now face will surely fail. We will win our freedom because the sacred heritage of our nation and the eternal will of God are embodied in our echoing demands."

Some forty years after the protests, Alabama Governor Bob Riley in April 2006 signed the "Rosa Parks Act" setting up a process to pardon those who were arrested for violating the state's segregation-era laws.

As in most of the big civil rights confrontations in the South, Birmingham had its staging area. There, it was Kelly Ingram Park. On one corner was the Baptist church; on another was the A.G. Gaston Motel. The block-square park was surrounded by small businesses and modest homes. In the days of the Birmingham Movement, this spot became the window through which the world saw Birmingham on television screens—a twenty-inch square view of life in a troubled Southern city.

A group of African American anti-segregation demonstrators run for safety as they are sprayed with high-pressure water from fire hoses during a civil rights march on May 3, 1963, in Birmingham, Alabama. Photo: © Bettmann-Corbis

Fire hoses and leashed police dogs were brought in to contain the blacks, keeping them within the confines of the park and away from downtown. Bull Connor and his police were there to see it happened that way. They were effective except for one time when several hundred blacks broke through the lines and swarmed downtown, shouting, singing, and scaring the wits out of shoppers. At one point James Bevel, the Mississippi field secretary of the SCLC, borrowed a police bullhorn when youngsters became too exuberant and reminded them of their commitment to peace.

Accounts of high-pressure fire hoses knocking children down and washing them into gutters, and of snarling dogs, served to fill the nation—and particularly the Congress and the White House—with revulsion and shock. In actual fact, as I witnessed it, most of the time children in that park were having a lark of a good time, taunting police, hiding behind trees, leaping out to be water-sprayed—at a safe distance—and jeering at police dogs that were held tightly on short leashes by their handlers. When it came to serious crowd control, however—when there was an effort by demonstrators to break out of the park—the water was turned on full force, and men, women, and children were cut down like match sticks. Several were bitten by dogs.

Alabama Governor George Wallace rushed the National Guard to Birmingham at one point to control downtown rioting. "I'm beginning to tire of agitators," the governor said.

Birmingham also made good use of a squat, ugly armored vehicle that looked like a cake box on wheels. It was effective in clearing the streets, herding demonstrators before its businesslike front end.

There were more serious concerns in Birmingham than children in a park. Bombs damaged Gaston's motel, as well as the home of black attorney Arthur Shores, who was active in the racial cause. The high ground on which his home sat became known as Dynamite Hill, it was hit so often. Each new incident sent crowds of demonstrators into the streets. There was one particularly brutal event, but no casualties resulted. Two explosive charges were placed on cleared ground in the black section of town, timed to go off fifteen minutes apart. The first apparently was a decoy, designed to draw a crowd when it exploded. The second was filled with shrapnel. For unexplainable reasons, the crowd that usually swarmed to a bombing scene failed to materialize, and the second explosion hurled its deadly pieces of metal onto an empty street.

Dynamite was easily accessible in Birmingham, a city built by the mines that surround it. Over a five-year period, there were at least twenty-five racial bombings. Most, however, were intended to frighten rather than to kill.

The nation's television screens left the impression that Birmingham was a city of violence from end to end. Actually, the black campaign rarely moved out of the Sixth Street Baptist Church, the nearby park, and the courtyard of the Gaston Motel, where King and his associates regularly talked with journalists. One day I left the noisy park for the federal court three blocks away and found people walking along unhurriedly, seemingly unaware of what was happening a few hundred feet away.

During a lull in the long demonstrations, I talked with A.G. Gaston, then seventy-one. He had traveled the world helping blacks get ahead. For his contributions in Africa, he was invited as an honored guest to a White House banquet for African leaders. He was in anguish over what was happening in his home city, but he remained firm in the conviction that blacks must—and could—pull themselves to the top. He believed that the destiny of blacks was to be in the mainstream of the nation. Yet, he acknowledged with some sadness that the Birmingham demonstrations had been necessary to focus the racial problems there. He had personally worked with blacks and whites in Birmingham to ease those tensions, but it had been very slow work.

"The Negro today is making great progress in civil rights, but it takes more than that," Gaston said. "It doesn't do any good to arrive at first-class citizenship if you arrive broke."

He felt that what blacks needed most was "a Martin Luther King of economics who will fire the people up like they are being fired up for civil rights." He observed that white people are quick to respect blacks who show responsibility with money.

"For instance," he recalled as we talked, "I had stock in two Birmingham banks that were considering a merger. Instead of voting by proxy, I decided to go to the stockholders' meeting. I didn't intend to say anything, but I heard others who owned a hundred or so shares doing all the talking. Well, I owned something like 1,500 shares in both the banks, and I decided I had better speak, too. Immediately, the white stockholders showed respect for this fellow who had so many shares.

"The only question I raised about the merger was whether the smaller bank might be gobbled up by the bigger one, and the Negro people would not get fair treatment. I was assured this would not happen, and I supported the merger. Now, the bank plans to put some Negro employees on the payroll right here in Birmingham. So, one of my rules for Negroes would be for them to start participating in affairs that concern them. They always leave it up to the other side to control the economy."

Throughout the ordeal of Birmingham, A.G. Gaston was working anonymously with black and white leadership to bring an end to the crisis. The decisive phase of those negotiations took place in the new Chamber of Commerce building just a few blocks from where the demonstrations ebbed and flowed. While police vans whined past with fresh crowds for the jail, a group of white leaders met behind closed doors of the Chamber building in search of a plan that would end the strife. It was called "The Committee of Seventy," known formally as the Senior Citizens Committee, not because of the members' ages—some of the youngest were in their thirties—but because they were some of the city's most influential citizens and represented all degrees of racial philosophy.

The meetings were held against a background of violence, but also with the knowledge that the trouble was costing business hard money. In one month city revenues, as measured by sales tax collections, declined by $1,765,400. People had stopped going downtown.

For almost two crucial days, the committee never emerged from its meeting place. Food was brought in, reminding some members of times when they had been closeted on juries. From time to time, the committee requested the appearance of a witness or a consultant. One of the latter was a highly respected Harvard-trained corporation lawyer by the name of Burke Marshall. He had joined the Kennedy administration as assistant attorney general in charge of the civil rights division.

Although Marshall had a natural shyness and scholarly appearance and wore horn-rimmed glasses, he was quite sure of himself and confident in the ability of responsible people on both sides of the racial fence to work out settlements. He was a master at bringing both sides into an atmosphere where they could talk together freely.

Marshall first discovered a great deal of emotion and various ideas about the basic issues. He helped the committee at the outset to sort out those issues. The white leadership, it turned out, was almost more concerned about the "outside agitators" who were stirring up trouble in Birmingham than in the actual demands of the blacks for desegregation of public facilities. That was an oft-related complaint throughout the South.

The committee represented about 80 percent of the business and industry in Birmingham, and Marshall spent much time talking with each member, since they represented so many elements of the city. Step by step an agreement was negotiated; then a six-member biracial group was chosen to put together the final draft.

In exchange for its organizers ending all demonstrations, the city and its businesses would, in stages, desegregate public eating places, restrooms, and drinking fountains at downtown department and variety stores; upgrade job opportunities; establish permanent communications between black and white leadership; and release without punishment the hundreds of prisoners who had been arrested during the demonstrations. The agreement was signed by all parties on May 10, 1963.

Some blacks distrusted the whites, recalling that many previous promises were broken. Martin Luther King, Jr., urged them to have faith, pointing out that "the political power structure always responds to the economic power structure."

The end of the dramatic Birmingham episode of the civil rights movement came almost unceremoniously. It had been agreed that King, the Reverend Fred Shuttlesworth, and the Reverend Ralph Abernathy would make the announcement at a news conference in the parking area of Gaston Motor Lodge. At the scheduled time, Shuttlesworth was missing. No amount of cajoling by the impatient press would persuade King to make the announcement without him, for Shuttlesworth at the time was head of the local action group that was pressing for the racial concessions. King knew that without his physical presence, the agreement would not stick.

Shuttlesworth finally was discovered in an upstairs room of the motel, clad in blue pajamas, and stretched out in his bed as though nothing of importance was happening. Either because he didn't feel well, or because of pique over being upstaged by the other "outside" blacks, Shuttlesworth was planning even in his moment of victory to demonstrate through his absence that he did not trust the settlement. He finally succumbed to King's persuasion, came downstairs, and the announcement was made as planned. Before that news conference was over, Shuttlesworth was taken by ambulance to a hospital, suffering from after effects of having been knocked flat by a fire hose during the demonstration in the park.

Two nights after the settlement, Gaston's motel and the home of King's brother were heavily damaged by dynamite. Even with this new violence against him, Gaston stood firm for peace and negotiation in Birmingham. "You use soldiers to win the war, but you use diplomats to win the peace," he said. "You never win anything if you go to the peace table with a gun in your hands."

Not only did Gaston favor communication with the whites of Birmingham, but conciliation. "You know, I took one of these courses that is supposed to show you how to make friends," the black leader said. "I guess I learned one lesson from it; that was to always let the other fellow save face even after you beat him."

Before the dust cleared in the two latest blasts, President Kennedy rushed three thousand riot control troops to bases close to Birmingham. He was taking no chances because the local government had not yet agreed to the biracial truce worked out by the business leaders. This was a critical stage; a moderate city government had just been elected, but had not been formally seated due to challenges in court by the recently ousted hard line officials. The slender thread of trust between black and white held, sparing the steel city a new racial outburst. This time the federal force was not needed.

One of the saddest tragedies of the mid-60s now occurred in Birmingham. During the weeks of the black campaign to break down segregation barriers, I watched as crowds of youngsters emerged from rallies in the Sixteenth Street Baptist Church, walked a block, and jumped into police vans, happily singing to jail at the behest of their adult leaders.

The long and bitter Birmingham demonstrations had ended without serious injury. On September 15, 1963, a quiet Sunday morning, I returned to news headquarters in Atlanta and was unpacking my car when word came that dynamite had ripped open the basement of Sixteenth Street Baptist Church, where just a week before I had sat while hundreds of demonstrators heard Dr. Martin Luther King, Jr., promise with outstretched arms that "we shall overcome." The Sunday School was in the basement of the church.

Denise McNair, eleven, Cynthia Wesley, Addie Mae Collins, and Carol Robertson, all fourteen, were in their Sunday School department donning choir robes when an explosive was lobbed into the church from a speeding car. The bodies of the four children were removed from the rubble by shocked white firemen and policemen, working side by side with black rescuers. In the debris a crumpled piece of paper was found with these words in a childish scrawl: "Dear God, we are sorry for the times we were so unkind."

The murders devastated the weary Birmingham community, white and black. All the energies of King and other leaders were required to prevent the city's blacks from rioting. The Birmingham agreement held.

Dr. Martin Luther King, Jr., holds a picture of three missing civil rights workers, Michael Schwerner, James Chaney, and Andrew Goodman (left to right) during a press conference on December 4, 1964. The bodies of the three men were later found near Philadelphia, Mississippi. Photo: © Bettmann-Corbis

CHAPTER 8

1964–Medgar Evers Slain; Three Civil Rights Volunteers Killed

"An unlearned carpenter of my acquaintance once said in my hearing: 'There is very little difference between one man, and another; but what little there is, is very important.' This distinction seems to me to go to the root of the matter."

—William James

Those involved in the civil rights movement had their own ideas of the movers and shakers in their campaign. In my opinion, they were not only the "leaders" of the dramatic marches, the euphoric rallies, or those with political pull at the highest levels of government. They were the valiant few who slugged it out in the trenches long before any reinforcements came, who moved into hostile towns of the South years before an organized movement for changing the racial status quo was conceived, and who stood up—lonely and, I suppose, afraid—for such simplicities as the right to vote.

Until the middle of the twentieth century, relatively few Southern blacks voted. Some blacks had voted in the segregated states for years without incident or protest, and whites sensitive to complaints about discrimination were eager to cite that fact. The fact was that the number of black voters was so few by comparison that their ballots made no difference. The Republican Party, seeking a way through the solid white Democratic wall in the South, had some success in the early to middle part of the century attracting blacks. But the political control in the South was not in the Republican camp at that time. It was a white Democratic South.

The Democratic white primary in my state of Georgia was the only vehicle for election to office—local, state, or national. The general election, where party had no weight, was much less significant than it later became. There were no black elected officials, and there was no way for most blacks to influence government to the slightest degree.

In this white-controlled political climate, the South for many years determined the leadership of the most important committees in the U.S. Senate, and to a lesser degree those in the House of Representatives. During this era, some of the outstanding senators and congressmen of the century served the nation well in the fields of finance, agriculture, and foreign policy. Through the seniority system, they kept key committee chairmanships locked up year after year. In close races back home, the veteran officeholders had a favorite and effective argument: "Now, you don't want me to lose my chairmanship." These powerful Southern officeholders, all white, were foursquare for racial segregation.

It was in this atmosphere that the National Association for the Advancement of Colored People worked patiently for years to educate and encourage blacks to take part in the election process that was guaranteed to them by the Constitution. One of the most difficult efforts was in Mississippi, where black voter registration was so low as to be meaningless. Before passage of the Voting Rights Act of 1965, 7 percent of legally eligible blacks were registered to vote in Mississippi. By comparison, more than 60 percent of eligible whites were registered. So, for the citizens whose skin was dark, Mississippi in some ways represented the worst side of life in the South.

In Mississippi—one of the last holdouts in the nation for total segregation of the races—the white population was for the most part, as I observed, gentle, friendly, peacefully disposed and law-abiding. These qualities even extended to relations with the black populace, but only under certain strict rules that had been clearly understood by white and black for many generations. Blacks had to "know their place"—not only in Mississippi but throughout the old South. It was the understanding that white rule, white customs, white desires, and white rights were the factors governing a peaceful life for blacks. In most places, there was trouble at best, death at worst, when these understandings were violated. The valiant few encountered both trouble and death.

Many well-meaning citizens, white and black, came through Alabama and Mississippi in those days to lend support to the civil rights movement. Some did not return home. William L. Moore, a white Baltimore, Maryland, policeman, was shot to death while walking on a road in northeast Alabama. He was carrying a sign that read: "Equal rights for all—Mississippi or bust."

This account of one reporter's passage through the complexities of the civil rights campaign does not intend to assess the rightness or wrongness of what these new strangers in the South did. Most of those I got to know seemed sincere—some over-zealous, foolish, and naive, but really dedicated to helping set right what they felt was wrong in the country. Many whites in the South hated them more than they did the black activists in their own region. History has proved so many times that man, when he is given truth before he can understand it or before he is ready to receive it, often turns violent. And that is what happened, tragically often. One of those tragedies occurred at Philadelphia, Mississippi.

The "Mississippi Summer Project" of 1964 was an interracial effort to persuade blacks to register to vote and to focus national attention on racial conditions. Hundreds of school- and college-age youth roamed the state, their mere presence fanning local outrage. They were unpaid volunteers, and some paid a heavy price.

Michael Schwerner, twenty-four, and Andrew Goodman, twenty, of New York City, both white, came South to work on the project. They joined James Chaney, twenty-two, who was black, of Meridian, Mississippi, to form a team. On June 20, the three were arrested for speeding near Philadelphia, a small farming town sixty-five miles northeast of Jackson, the state capital. Deputy Sheriff Cecil Price claimed they were kept overnight in jail, released the next day, taken to the edge of town, and told to leave the area. They soon disappeared.

Philadelphia became a rumor mill. Some said the missing youths were killed and their bodies dropped into the quicksand of Bogue Chitta Swamp near town, where they would never be found. The story everyone wanted to believe was that the whole thing was a hoax.

Patient young strangers turned up in Philadelphia: agents of the Federal Bureau of Investigation. They asked questions and looked for clues. On August 4, at the direction of the FBI, a bulldozer and a large earth-moving scoop were sent to Olen Burrage's new fish pond dam near town and put to work at a specific spot in the still-soft earthworks.

Bodies of the three civil rights workers were found buried twenty feet down from the top of the dam. The FBI, protecting its informers, would not say how it knew. The bodies had been dumped into a shallow hole at the bottom of the dam, and the unsuspecting contractor, in closing the middle of the four-hundred-foot project, had bulldozed loose earth onto the victims. All three had been shot. A family doctor reported that James Chaney had been savagely beaten with a blunt instrument or chain before his execution.

On December 4, 1964, exactly four months after discovery of the bodies, the FBI arrested twenty-one whites on federal conspiracy charges—including the sheriff and a deputy of Neshoba County, and a minister. An all-white federal court jury in Meridian, Mississippi, convicted seven on charges of conspiracy to murder. They included Chief Deputy Sheriff Cecil Price and Ku Klux Klan Wizard Sam Bowers. Sheriff Lawrence Rainey was acquitted. Bowers got a maximum sentence of ten years, Price six, the others three to ten years.

All Mississippians were not quiet about conditions in their state. Hazel Brannon Smith, a courageous white editor of weekly newspapers in Mississippi, suffered harassment, threats, and vandalism for editorials appearing in her papers in the 1950s. "Today in much of Mississippi we live in an atmosphere of fear," she wrote. "It hangs like a dark cloud over us, dominating almost every facet of public and private life. No one speaks freely any more for fear of being misunderstood. Editors, preachers, teachers and other professional people are affected by it, as well as business and industry. Almost every man and woman is afraid to try to do anything to promote good will and harmony between the races—afraid he or she will be taken as a mixer, or worse."

Although confronted with this kind of restrictive atmosphere, Mississippi blacks in the mid-twentieth century began to talk of registering to vote, considered the possibility of some day electing a black person to public office, determined to have better education, decided to become citizens with equal rights. Courage was required just to talk about such dreams.

Medgar Evers was a young man of such courage. He was born in the little Mississippi town of Decatur, forty miles east of Jackson. In 1950, at the age of twenty-five, he went to work for the National Association for the Advancement of Colored People. His job with the NAACP was persuading Mississippi blacks to register for voting.

The work of this young black native of Mississippi was difficult, slow, and dangerous. Between 1950 and 1960, largely through his efforts, the percentage of voter registration among blacks in Mississippi rose to just 5.2 percent of blacks legally eligible to vote. It was still by far the smallest percentage of black registration anywhere in the South.

In 1954, the year that the U. S. Supreme Court outlawed public school segregation, Evers was promoted to the position of Mississippi's first state field secretary of the NAACP. For the next nine years, he stayed at his post in a little office in Jackson, persuading and educating blacks about voter registration. Interestingly, in view of the attitude in Mississippi at the time, Evers began drawing a measure of respect from some in the white populace, and he was left alone to do his work. His voter registration effort was slow and frustrating, but it began to bear results.

Such work as his in Mississippi also began to have an effect in the nation's capital where voices—demanding voices—were heard for a strong new civil rights law. On June 11, 1963, President Kennedy addressed the nation by television and radio, proclaiming: "We are confronted primarily with a moral issue." The fires of frustration are burning in every city, North and South, where legal remedies are not at hand. Redress is sought in the streets, in demonstrations, parades and protests which create tensions and threaten violence—and threaten lives . . . We cannot say to 10 percent of the population that you can't have that right [to develop talents through education], that your children cannot have the chance to develop whatever talents they have, that the only way that they are going to get their rights is to go into the streets and demonstrate. I think we owe them and we owe ourselves a better country than that."

About midnight on the evening following the president's address in Washington, Medgar Evers returned to his home in Jackson from a voter registration meeting. He parked his automobile in the driveway of his residence, opened the car door, and stepped out. Almost immediately, a shot broke the midnight silence. Evers stumbled to the nearby kitchen door and fell mortally wounded; he lived only a few hours. He had long remarked that he was on "somebody's hit list" and in a television interview one year before his murder said "whenever my time comes, I am ready."

Roy Wilkins, Evers' boss at NAACP, called him "a martyr in the crusade for human liberty . . . The bullet that tore away his life tore away at the system and helped to signal its end. They can fiddle and they can throw a few more victims to the lions of repression and persecution, but Rome is burning and a new day is just over yonder."

President Kennedy wrote to the grieving widow: "The achievement of the goals he did so much to promote will enable the generations to follow to share fully and equally in the benefits and advantages our nation has to offer."

Jackson police who converged on the murder scene within minutes found a patch of weeds pressed down in a vacant lot within sight of Evers' frame and brick home. An army rifle with a Japanese telescopic sight was found in a clump of bushes.

The slain black leader's Masonic Hall funeral was a deeply emotional experience. His casket was almost hidden under flowers that flowed out on both sides of a long stage. A massed chorus of black singers filled much of the stage. The crowds of mourners came early. Murmurs drifted through the room as national civil rights figures arrived.

To report the story, I ordered a special telephone installed backstage. As the service began, I dialed the UPI number in Atlanta and said quietly, "I am ready to dictate."

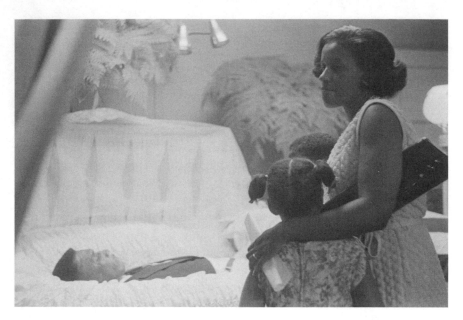

Myrlie Evers and her children view the body of slain civil rights leader Medgar
Evers during his funeral in Jackson, Mississippi. Murder charges against suspect
Byron de la Beckwith for the assassination of Medgar Evers were dropped after two
trials ended in mistrial, but he was convicted in 1994 and died in prison in 2001.
Photo: © Bettmann-Corbis

The news account of the memorial service began moving on the wires to UPI subscribers while the tributes were still in progress. This was an important civil rights development internationally, for Evers was the first "name" leader to pay with his life for his work in the black voter registration campaign. I felt almost detached from the charged atmosphere of the setting. As the long funeral service, replete with songs and eulogies, drew to a close, the chorus stood for a final hymn, filling the auditorium with the strains of the triumphant battle song of the civil rights movement, "We Shall Overcome." When the final verse began, the a cappella chorus was joined by twelve golden trumpets. It was too much; my dictation faltered, and I wept into the phone. I had an idea that the person taking dictation on the other end of the line wept, too. I saw tears of anguish on more than one white face that day.

Byron de la Beckwith, a white man, member of an old family in the Mississippi Delta country, was arrested on charges of killing Evers. He was tried twice before Mississippi juries, and both ended in mistrials because of deadlocked juries. He was released, a free man to pick up his activities.

Three years after the Evers slaying, Beckwith was one of six questioned in the firebombing of a home at the time of a Congressional hearing into Ku Klux Klan resurgence. All six refused to answer questions. In 1967 Beckwith unsuccessfully sought the Mississippi lieutenant governor's position. In 1973 he was arrested with a time bomb in his possession, and two years later in the New Orleans jury trial of the case, he was sentenced to five years in prison on conviction of transporting "a ticking time bomb" across state lines. He was freed on bond pending appeal and never served any time.

During the two trials for the Medgar Evers' killing, a thirty-seven-year-old prosecuting attorney in the Hinds County, Mississippi, judicial circuit, William Waller, fought doggedly to get a conviction. What he got was his first hate letter. "It came from Philadelphia in Pennsylvania," he told me with sad surprise.

The news media, including a black reporter for the *New York Post*, sat in the balcony of the Hinds County courthouse to report the proceedings. In the corridors during trial recess, it was quickly obvious that most sentiment among white spectators was not on the prosecutor's side; it was generally talked about town that Beckwith would be acquitted in short order.

The fact that the jury deadlocked, caused by some members holding out for a conviction, was considered a major victory for Waller, and a great surprise to most local observers. This was a small part of the revolution of change in Mississippi. Human rights advances rarely came full bloom through a single experience, but such agonies as the murder of Medgar Evers did have an effect on the overall picture.

In 1989, Hinds County Assistant District Attorney Bobby DeLaughter reopened the case, and in 1994 a twelve-member jury that included eight blacks convicted Beckwith of first-degree murder in the slaying of Evers. Beckwith died in prison in 2001.

Charles Evers succeeded his murdered brother in the Mississippi NAACP office, and in 1968 led a biracial coalition from Mississippi to the Democratic National Convention, which unseated the state's all-white delegation. The next year, Charles Evers was elected mayor of Fayette, Mississippi.

One week after Medgar Evers was killed, President Kennedy revised an earlier—and much weaker—civil rights request and sent to Congress a greatly expanded measure which became the heart of a sweeping new national Civil Rights Act. In addition to earlier proposals to insure voting rights, the new bill addressed the most controversial and, by many, most feared provision: public accommodations.

Representative Emanuel Celler, New York Democrat, chairman of the House Judiciary Committee, said in urging passage of the 1963 legislation: "In Birmingham, Alabama, in Greenwood, Mississippi, police clubs and bludgeons, fire hoses and dogs have been used on defenseless schoolchildren who were marching and singing hymns in protest of denial of civil rights . . . If we could put ourselves in place of the Negro and experience, day by day, the humiliations which the Negro faces, there would be no difficulty in enacting strong civil rights legislation."

Attorney General Robert F. Kennedy, the president's brother, testified that the new administration measure would "go a long way toward redeeming the pledges upon which this Republic was founded — pledges that all are created equal, that they are endowed equally with unalienable rights and are entitled to equal opportunity in the pursuit of their daily lives."

Representative W. J. Bryan Dorn, South Carolina Democrat, urged Congress not to consider civil rights legislation "as a result of mob violence and demonstrations and agitation." Dorn said he grew "tired of people who are always talking about their rights."

Representative Joe D. Waggonner, Jr., Louisiana Democrat, said he had no apology to make for believing that "it is neither illegal nor immoral to prefer the peaceful and orderly separation of the races without discrimination or rancor of any kind."

One of the most effective testifiers for the new legislation was Roy Wilkins, executive secretary of the National Association for the Advancement of Colored People. His organization over the years spent many thousands of dollars in legal battles for minority rights and came reluctantly to the side of street demonstrators by the 1960s.

Answering the theme of critics that blacks were making steady progress without the demonstrations, and that they should be patient, Wilkins said blacks were citizens of the United States, entitled to federal protection against "the infringement of their rights," that they had done "everything for their country that has been asked of them, even to standing back and waiting patiently, under pressure and persecution, for that which they should have had at the very beginning of their citizenship."

Wilkins said that blacks were no longer willing to wait in patience and that, as a matter of fact, the current racial demonstrations were in large part a reaction to "the indifference toward, and outright defiance of" the 1954 Supreme Court school desegregation decision.

The administration's bill called for a four-year extension of the Civil Rights Commission, and this turned out to be the only part of the legislation passed by the Congress in 1963. As the debate subsided, street action escalated, spreading to more than eight hundred cities, large and small, before year's end.

Black leaders, keeping up their emphatic demands for a stronger law, seemed not dismayed at the small victory in 1963, believing that from the 158 pieces of civil rights legislation generated by the debate, a major new law would emerge the next year. The job of Congress was now to find a way to merge all those bills into a package that would be approved by liberals and moderates, and also would be accepted by conservative Southern Democrats.

Senator Jacob J. Javits, the New York Republican, reminded his colleagues: "To understand fully what this legislation is about, one need only for a moment put himself in the position of the Negro who, walking into a restaurant or a hotel or a store, must first look around apprehensively to see whether or not he or she is welcome. I have seen this human tragedy a thousand times myself."

The sort of tragedy Senator Javits referred to was something that Medgar Evers lived with every day, but, because he knew what the ballot would mean to the black people of Mississippi, he never let himself be drawn into the side roads of the civil rights drive. Carefully, persuasively, almost methodically and with documentation, he sought to convince blacks one by one and in small, sometimes apprehensive groups, that they must become registered voters as soon as possible.

At the Medgar Evers funeral, Roy Wilkins stressed that others must take up the task and carry the demand for the ballot to the seat of government.

During the heated congressional debate that summer of 1963, a statement was issued by Ivan Allen, white mayor of Atlanta, member of a distinguished old Southern family, and a prominent business and civil leader before he entered politics. Allen, who coined a slogan for Atlanta, "a city too busy to hate," called segregation "slavery's stepchild" and urged Congress to pass a public accommodations law. If that were not done, the mayor argued, it would "amount to an endorsement of private businesses setting up an entirely new status of discrimination throughout the country. Cities like Atlanta might slip backward. Hotels and restaurants that have already taken this issue upon themselves and opened their doors might find it convenient to go back to the old status."

When Ivan Allen entered the mayor's office, one of his first moves was to make the place accessible to everyone, and that meant leaving the door always open.

He had all the stiff-back chairs removed and replaced with comfortable cane-bottom rockers of the type often seen in those days on Southern verandas. He was a sensible and sensitive city executive, a big factor in Atlanta's generally smooth transition to desegregation. He maintained contact with all sides on every issue.

A measure of Allen's sensitivity came on a Sunday in 1962 when more than one hundred Atlanta art lovers, on a trip to France, were killed on take-off from Orly Airport in Paris. Allen was operating a tractor at his farm near Atlanta when the news was brought to him. The tractor was left in the field, and the mayor rushed to the airport for a flight to Paris. He wanted to report from first-hand knowledge to families of the victims.

The South was blessed with many men—and women—like Allen who, beneath their generations-long habits and traditions, had a sense of rightness and justice. These inner traits helped make possible the transition that moved blacks closer to society's mainstream.

This photo, taken from the top of the Lincoln Memorial, shows how the March on Washington participants jammed the area in front of the Memorial and on either side of the Reflecting Pool on August 28, 1963. They are massed at the pool all the way back to the Washington Monument. Photo: © Bettmann-Corbis

CHAPTER 9

1963–Lincoln Memorial Echoes Freedom

"I have a dream."   —Dr. Martin Luther King, Jr.

"I dream'd in a dream I saw a city invincible to the attacks of the whole of the rest of the earth, I dream'd that was the new city of Friends."

—Walt Whitman

While the civil rights oratory droned on in Congress, black leaders sought a means of bringing all the racial organizations—some with widely divergent views—together as one force for civil rights. It was A. Phillip Randolph who conceived the big idea of 1963: a summer demonstration in Washington, D.C., the nation's capital, the seat of government, the domicile of Congress, the place that the president had promised to make the most integrated city in America. The purpose of Randolph's plan was to dramatize black appeals for better jobs and job opportunities.

Randolph had been in the civil rights business for a long, long time. He was president of the Negro American Labor Council, and the Brotherhood of Sleeping Car Porters, one of the most esteemed labor unions in the United States. His was a black union, representing the porters in whose care were the sleeping cars that crisscrossed the country on rails. His was a union of great dignity, a proper reflection of the pride that was the hallmark of the members' service to passengers in the heyday of train transportation.

At first, blacks were less than enthusiastic about a Washington demonstration. They felt the civil rights movement could not risk the shame of failure, and that this was a high-risk venture despite their high regard for Randolph. The logistics of organizing such a demonstration were too complex, they reasoned; besides, where would all those people go to the bathroom in downtown Washington? There was also strong opposition by official Washington. The Justice Department, the president, and congressional leaders were against it.

Of major concern was the knowledge that members of George Lincoln Rockwell's American Nazi Party would be on hand threatening to break up the march. Rockwell's "army" was headquartered in nearby Virginia and had been somewhat active, but mostly vocal thus far, in opposition to the aspirations of black Americans.

But Randolph, long known for his determined streak, was adamant. Such a symbolic demonstration was his style, and he would go ahead if he were the only one to organize it. Catching onto the idea, Martin Luther King, Jr., proposed that all civil rights organizations—often at odds over strategy and purpose—join forces in a massive march for "jobs and freedom" in the nation's capital. It was pure symbolism. Roy Wilkins of the NAACP spoke of "demonstrating with our bodies" that blacks were united.

During the planning stages of this event, I had an interview with Wilkins, one of the steadiest of the civil rights leadership. "This is a concrete expression from the grass roots," he said. "This is not King and Wilkins interpreting. These are the people, all in one place, in person, saying to the government that they have given up their pay for a day or two, and that they have lost sleep and comforts to come to Washington to say they want first-class citizenship."

Reluctantly at first, and then with gathering enthusiasm as they were swept up in the extraordinary significance of the event, other civil rights organizations fell into line. They began to realize that, in this summer of 1963, the Washington march represented the only unifying plan for the movement—a definite effort that had a date, time, place, and goal. August 28 was decided upon. The marshaling point would be the spacious esplanade around the Washington Monument. The destination would be the steps of the imposing Lincoln Memorial about a mile to the west.

Bayard Rustin, King's informal adviser in his own civil rights campaign, a man who had a reputation for controlling crowds, was brought in as chief strategist, and the organization of the march began. Suggestions for raising travel money, instructions (travel light, bring enough food for one day, and don't drink much water) directions (how to reach the Washington Monument by plane, train, and bus)—all began turning up at scores of civil rights headquarters. Press releases estimated the prospective crowd weeks before August: 40,000, 50,000, 60,000, 100,000. The figure kept escalating and being questioned. Who really knew whether the Montgomery group, as an example, would send twenty or one hundred?

In official Washington, no chances regarding security were taken. All police leaves were canceled. State police in states bordering the District of Columbia beefed up patrols. The military moved armed troops into alert encampment at strategic spots around the capital. Finally, the sanitation department moved in portable toilets (paid for by the march organizers) and picked up from the march area every stone large enough to be effectively thrown in anger.

News organizations moved to town for the most elaborate coverage ever of a domestic event up to that time. A spokesman for Columbia Broadcasting System, which handled the main television pool operation for the march, said it was the most ambitious television coverage in the United States to be produced outside a studio. At least forty television cameras were aimed at the proceedings. Deputy Police Chief Howard V. Covell told us at a news briefing that, up to the time of the current event, he had issued 1,200 police department press badges in his thirty-three years in the department. "For this one story, we have issued 1,537 passes, and I have been advised to get another 500 printed," he said.

August 28 was fair, hot, and humid—a typical Washington summer day. At the White House six blocks to the north of the monument, the tourists began lining up early for the standard walk-through of the visitors' floors. But on this day, there seemed to be fewer school children and charter buses than usual.

During the previous night, carpenters had erected a large platform not far from the monument. This was for the entertainers whose mission was to attract the attention of the arriving crowds, holding them together until the march stepped off, scheduled at 11 a.m. At 8 a.m., the monument esplanade was almost deserted except for a few television technicians checking out equipment on a smaller stand, a policeman here and there, small groups of curious onlookers.

If this was the marshaling area for a massive demonstration, where were the people? As the morning wore on, the march leaders became increasingly apprehensive. The crowd was simply not materializing in the five- and six-figure numbers needed to call the project a success.

But there were enough people around to be entertained, and Hollywood, Broadway, and recording personalities belted it out. Unnoticed by most of the waiting marchers, a small drama was enacted on a green slope near the monument where George Lincoln Rockwell's Nazi "storm troopers" were assembled, attired in brown uniforms with black and white swastika armbands.

Washington police were under orders to play it cool on this day. Soft talk and gentle persuasion were the weapons of law and order, not handcuffs and paddy wagons. But how do you handle a group that has proclaimed ahead of time that its mission was to disrupt and break up the march to the Lincoln Memorial? "Surround them," was the order to officers on the Rockwell assignment. Ingenious.

Unobtrusively, almost in a loitering posture, one hundred police officers stationed themselves around the "Nazis." Wherever the counter-demonstrators moved, the circle of officers also moved. The plan so disconcerted the Rockwell group that they never moved off the green slope and finally packed up and went home to Virginia without getting close to the marchers.

By 10 a.m., one hour before the march was to begin, the crowd was up to perhaps twenty thousand. Soon, I calculated, it would be necessary to telephone my news bureau and report that the event might be routine. But first, I would check with the District police. It was a good thing to do. What were they picking up from the surrounding countryside by radio and planes? Police reported that every highway leading into Washington from every direction was jammed bumper to bumper; bus stations, air terminals, railroad stations were packed. From the air, it appeared that everything moving that morning was moving toward Washington.

The entertainers sang on and on; hawkers of ice cream sandwiches eased the pain of waiting; some in the crowd tried out the new toilets; and on came the people until the time of the march. When the announced moment came, this great throng, now numbering many thousands, could no longer be contained. With no disorder and no signals, people began to move slowly, like a stream unleashed seeking its course. The march leaders were hurriedly assembled and rushed to the front of the column and, after a brief pause for ceremony and pictures of this historic event, the multitude moved again toward the Lincoln Memorial.

It was a stirring scene, this lineup of powerful men, united in simplicity and neighborliness for a few hours by the enormity of this event, and behind them the people.

Even as the leaders lined up across Fifteenth Street—arms crossed, hands held in one long front column—they had no idea how many stood behind them. The architects of the U.S. civil rights movement were all there, save one who was in jail, together now, strength surging from man to man. Among them were Martin Luther King, Jr., of the Southern Christian Leadership Conference; Roy Wilkins, of the National Association for the Advancement of Colored People; Whitney Young, Jr., of the National Urban League;

A. Phillip Randolph, of the Brotherhood of Sleeping Car Porters; John Lewis, of the Student Non-Violent Coordinating Committee; Rabbi Joachim Prinz, American Jewish Congress; Bayard Rustin, the march strategist; Dr. Eugene Carson Blake, of the National Council of Churches; Walter Reuther, president of the United Automobile Workers Union; and Dr. Ralph Bunche of the United Nations Secretariat.

"Anyone who cannot understand the significance of your presence here today is blind and deaf," Bunche told the crowd.

James Farmer, leader of the Congress of Racial Equality, missed the Washington march. He was in jail in Louisiana for his civil rights activity there. But he sent a message, read by Floyd McKissick of the NAACP, which said: "We will not stop until the dogs stop biting us in the South, and the rats stop biting us in the North."

And who were these marchers? By police estimates, they numbered almost two hundred thousand men and women, some hobbling on crutches, others in wheelchairs; whites, blacks, and Asians, many sore of feet from having walked and hitchhiked across the country to reach this place; some already hungry because they brought no food. But it was a happy crowd; a friendly crowd; a crowd that for this day was at peace with itself; a generous crowd, for brown bag lunches were shared on the way to their destination; and it was a dedicated and committed crowd. There was a goal up ahead beyond the blue reflecting pool—Abe Lincoln himself looking down from his marble height on this remarkable scene.

So, they marched the eleven long blocks to the Lincoln Memorial, and there they listened, they sang, and many wept. Emotions were high for these people who had come from city streets and from small towns and rural Southern countryside. The tightly packed multitude extended down the Lincoln Memorial steps, to the reflecting pool where weary listeners sat on the edge and dabbled aching feet in the cool water. Their leaders came one by one to the microphone on the memorial steps and spoke words of hope and promise of a brighter future.

John Lewis remarked toward the end of that memorable day: "We will march through the South . . . But we will march with the spirit of love and the spirit of dignity that we have shown here today."

Finally came the last speaker, Dr. Martin Luther King, Jr. Never had he participated in such a demonstration as this one that Phillip Randolph had conceived. He stood there for a moment surveying the throng, and then began to speak in that rhythmic delivery with the rounded-off words that pulled people to him as though a magnet were imbedded in every word.

Merriman Smith and I were covering for UPI, and we had seats on a special press platform just to the left of the speakers. We had been handed advance texts of all principal speeches, and we followed these closely to make certain we caught any deviation from the prepared versions. No speaker had changed a word up to now, and King was no exception. His was not a spectacular speech, far from his best.

There were a few bursts of applause, but it was a rather quiet reception for this man who could spellbind such a crowd. It seemed that these people were growing weary of speeches. King went through the text just as he had written it in a hotel room session that had lasted almost all of the previous night. We had already dictated to our office what we considered the significant portions of the big march story, including King's prepared speech. So far as we were concerned, the story at the Lincoln Memorial was about buttoned up.

Completing his prepared remarks, King laid the papers aside. Then he raised his arms slowly as though to encircle that mass of humanity. There was hardly a pause in his delivery as he went from text to inspiration:

"I say to you today, my friends, that in spite of the difficulties and frustrations of the moment, I still have a dream."

Smitty, who covered the White House for UPI and was one of the best word merchants in the profession, almost leaped into the air as he grabbed for the King text and a note pad. "My God, he's going off the cuff," Smith rumbled. I picked up the direct line telephone that had been installed for our use and told the Washington news desk: "New lead coming on march."

King's eloquence, which I had heard sway crowds in Mississippi and Alabama churches, suddenly knew no bounds. In the multitude before him, many who were restless, weary, and leaving for home, turned back to face the speaker, instantly transported to a new summit of hope and exhilaration. King could do that to people.

At the height of the civil rights thrust into the Deep South, I had watched in fascination as King calmed angry blacks who wanted to go out and tear up the town. He was a master at reading the mood of his "children"—holding them inside churches until they were "spiritually ready," as he put it, to turn the other cheek to whatever violence they might encounter in the streets.

King's great speeches had a magnetic rhythm—a measured beat, a modulation in delivery that shifted for emphasis from gentle tones to strong. Themes were repeated, over and over—underscoring, driving home important points. There was a kind of signal, handed down from religious revivals and transferred to this religion-oriented activist movement, that indicated

*Dr. Martin Luther King, Jr., delivers his "I Have a Dream" speech in front of the
Lincoln Memorial during the Freedom March on Washington on August 28, 1963.
Photo: © Bettmann-Corbis*

when King was in contact with his audience. The signal usually began as a
low hum, loading to a drawn-out, soulful "Yes"; it was a mounting tide of
emotion that ended with clapping, cheering, shouting, and weeping. It was
so on this day in Washington. The signal came from the people.

". . . It is a dream deeply rooted in the American dream," King said.

"Yes," came the first signal from somewhere down in that great congregation between the memorial and the reflecting pool. King heard the response,
and his voice took on the vibrant tone that was so much a hallmark of his civil
rights oratory.

"I have a dream that one day this nation will rise up and live out the true
meaning of its creed: 'We hold these truths to be self-evident; that all men
are created equal.' I have a dream ['Yes. Yes.'] that one day on the red hills of
Georgia the sons of former slaves and the sons of former slaveholders will be
able to sit down together at the table of brotherhood. I have a dream ['Say it!
Say it!'] that one day even the state of Mississippi, a desert state sweltering
with the heat of injustice and oppression, will be transformed into an oasis
of freedom and justice."

A woman who fainted in the crowd during the March on Washington is assisted by police officers and National Guardsmen. Photo: © Bettmann-Corbis

"I have a dream—[the crowd is now shouting and cheering, clapping and waving their arms with every mention of this new theme word 'dream']—that my four little children will one day live in a nation where they will not be judged by the color of their skin, but by the content of their character.

"I have a dream today . . ."

We were writing furiously, trying to get down his words, because there were no notes, no text for this one—only King at his best. We had no time to look at the crowd's reaction, but it was unnecessary. The reaction could be heard and felt like something visceral, now sweeping up almost in a sob from the depths of many hearts, making the long trek to Washington at last worthwhile for them. A woman in the dense crowd fainted; strong hands lifted her aloft, and she was passed above the heads of the throng to an emergency vehicle on the perimeter.

"I have a dream that one day the state of Alabama, whose governor's lips are presently dripping with the words of interposition and nullification, will be transformed into a situation where little black boys and black girls will be able to join hands with little white boys and white girls and walk together as sisters and brothers . . ."

It is difficult for the present generation to comprehend the effect of what King was saying. It is so different today. With black players on Southern athletic teams, with blacks in the legislatures and in the branches of state and local governments, and with blacks in white schools and business, states of the old South do not appear to be much different from other states. But in 1963, it was another story.

The speaker paused for an instant that seemed forever. I was only about fifty feet away when I quickly glanced up at him. He held not a piece of paper, no speech. His face was riveted on the stunned crowd. He seemed to be reaching for the last obedient servant in his audience. In this single pause, he brought up a different voice, brought forth a different leader. Then, he spoke.

". . . I have a dream today," Dr. King said. "I have a dream that one day every valley shall be exalted, every hill and mountain shall be made low; the rough places will be made plain, and the crooked places will be made straight; and the glory of the Lord shall be revealed, and all flesh shall see it together.

"And if America is to be a great nation, this must become true. So, let freedom ring from the prodigious hilltops of New Hampshire. ['Yes, Lord.'] Let freedom ring from the mighty mountains of New York. ['Yes, Yes, Yes.'] Let freedom ring from the heightening Alleghenies of Pennsylvania. Let freedom ring from the snowcapped Rockies of Colorado. ['Amen!'] Let freedom ring from every hill and mole hill of Mississippi. From every mountainside, let freedom ring.

"When we let freedom ring, when we let it ring from every village and every hamlet, from every state and every city, we will be able to speed up that day when all of God's children, black men and white men, Jews and Gentiles, Protestants and Catholics, will be able to join hands and sing in the words of the old Negro spiritual: 'Free at last! Free at last!' Thank God Almighty, we are free at last!"

A hush fell over the vast audience as King completed his message and gathered up the pages of his prepared address that no one would remember. And then the silence suddenly was broken; released emotion surged up from that crowd at the Lincoln Memorial. Thousands wept without shame. It was a mighty electric charge that would flow back to Mississippi and Alabama and rekindle flagging spirits. It flowed into the White House six blocks away and opened the doors that had been closed. The president of the United States, John Fitzgerald Kennedy, sent word to the demonstration leaders: "I will see you."

James Reston wrote in the *New York Times* of the King speech: "It was King who, near the end of the day, touched the vast audience. Until then, the pilgrimage was merely a great spectacle. Only those marchers from the embattled towns of the old Confederacy had anything like the old crusading zeal. For many, the day seemed an adventure, a long outing in the late summer sun—part liberation from home, part Sunday school picnic, part political convention, and part fish fry.

"But Dr. King brought them alive in the late afternoon with a peroration that was an anguished echo from all the old American reformers: Roger Williams calling for religious liberty, Sam Adams calling for political liberty, old man Thoreau denouncing coercion, William Lloyd Garrison demanding emancipation, and Eugene V. Debs crying for economic equality. Dr. King echoed them all. 'I have a dream,' he cried, again and again."

The headline in the *Times* that day read: "Capital Is Occupied by a Gentle Army."

President Kennedy addresses the nation by radio and television from his office in the White House on June 11, 1963, in the wake of the crisis over admitting two African Americans to the University of Alabama. He said that every American should stop and "examine his conscience" about the rights of Negroes. Photo: © Bettmann-Corbis

CHAPTER 10

1963-1964–Kennedy Slain; Johnson Takes Up Fight

"The air was like a furnace."

—Anonymous description of black and white leaders meeting
in St. Augustine

*"The bravest are surely those who have the clearest vision of what is
before them, glory and danger alike, and yet notwithstanding go out
to meet it."*

—Thucydides, 460-400 B.C.

Against a backdrop of daily racial demonstrations, President Kennedy's attitude toward the civil rights cause changed dramatically in the summer of 1963. Earlier, he had been roundly criticized for what liberals called a "thin" 1963 civil rights proposal, enunciated in his January State-of-the-Union address to Congress. These critics decried the Kennedy plan as a mere tidying-up of already existing laws.

On June 19, the president moved boldly to stand in the full spotlight and behind the most far-reaching civil rights aims. Broadening earlier proposals, he now asked that the rights of all Americans be extended to public accommodations. This had become the most insistent demand of blacks and was drawing great resistance from segregationists, as well as from many in Congress.

The president's new agenda was a proposed law that would "guarantee to all persons, regardless of race, color, religion or national origin, the full and equal enjoyment of the goods, services and facilities of hotels, motels, or other public places providing lodging to transient guests; motion picture houses, theaters, sports arenas, exhibition halls or other public entertainment; places whose sources of entertainment moved in interstate commerce; and retail shops, gas stations, restaurants or other establishments where goods are held out to the public for sale, use, rent, or hire . . . ," provided those services are afforded to interstate travelers and "substantially affect" interstate commerce.

A provision of the new proposal would "permit anyone who is denied access to these accommodations because of race to sue in court for preventive relief through a civil injunction" and would "permit the Attorney General to bring such a suit" on a written complaint from aggrieved parties.

While Congress deliberated, argued, compromised, and prayed through the summer and fall of 1963, President Kennedy hit the trail like a campaigner to seek public support for the legislation from anyone who would listen, North or South. He was in the midst of this activity when a fellow Democrat, Texas Governor John F. Connally, asked the president to ride with him in a motorcade through the streets of Dallas, Texas, as a demonstration of political unity.

The president agreed to make the Dallas trip. On November 22, while riding in the back seat of an open car with his wife, Jacqueline, and Connally, he was shot from ambush by a sniper and was pronounced dead thirty minutes later.

Ninety-eight minutes after Kennedy's death, Vice President Lyndon Johnson was sworn in as the thirty-sixth President of the United States. Five days later, in his first address to the Congress as chief executive, he urged that the Kennedy civil rights legislation be promptly approved.

"No memorial oration or eulogy could more eloquently honor President Kennedy's memory than the earliest possible passage of the civil rights bill for which he fought so long," the new president said. "We have talked long enough in this country about civil rights. We have talked for one hundred years or more. It is time now to write the next chapter—and to write it in the books of law."

By year's end, the civil rights legislation was in the House Rules Committee, headed for expected House approval in some form in early 1964. But lengthy and bitter debate in the Senate was anticipated, and the fate of the "symbolic heart" of the legislation—public accommodations—was in doubt. The tragedy of Dallas had not changed all minds in Congress on the civil rights issue.

In the midst of the most urgent and critical discussions, it was ever thus that man feels compelled to go through the exercise of formality. And so the amenities were not overlooked on the opening day of congressional debate on the new civil rights bill.

The chaplain, the Reverend Barnard Braskamp, was called to the well of the House for prayer: "May we earnestly covet and lay hold of those ideals and principles which will make for the health of our own individual souls and the spiritual welfare of all mankind . . . May we be willing to build a more humane social order where all the members of the human family shall live together in peace and honor and seek one another's good and happiness."

Among first orders of business in the House that day was receipt of a routine message from the Senate that had passed without amendment a House bill to provide for the striking of medals to commemorate the 200th anniversary of the founding of St. Louis, Missouri.

Only then came the House oratory on the civil rights bill. The debate ebbed and flowed, like tides pounding against the walls of the chamber.

Representative Peter Rodino of New Jersey argued that the legislation "will achieve more to advance the cause of civil rights than all the governmental actions of the last one hundred years put together." He said it would hasten desegregation of public schools and public facilities; in many parts of the nation would give blacks confidence to sit at a lunch counter—"how modest an advance that is"—take an overnight drive, or buy a theater ticket without fear.

Representative Claude Forrester of Georgia, speaking against the bill: "The great trouble is you forget, sirs, that the Constitution gives you the right to discriminate. Did you ever turn to your Constitution and read that 14th Amendment that you put so much stock by? [It] guarantees to you equal protection of the law."

Forrester condemned the legislation as "the most dictatorial ever submitted to a Congress." He cited recent House passage of a bill providing counsel for indigent defendants. Now, he said, "we see the legal machinery of the United States thrown against one poor, little, puny one-horse farmer who wants his soil bank check and he cannot get it because somebody in a bureau down here or some fool rule said he is guilty of discrimination. How crazy can we get?"

Many of the speeches were for the benefit of constituents back home. Most House members already felt the bill would pass in that chamber, but recognized that the Senate was in doubt. Yet, speak they did, in great volume under a rule that on this legislation every member who desired to speak could do so. Then, when all the talk in the House ceased, members put themselves on the line with a roll call vote. The bill passed by a margin of 290-130.

The South was relatively quiet for awhile, but about this time a new and dramatic event began to unfold in the picturesque Atlantic seacoast resort of St. Augustine, Florida, the nation's oldest city. A mix of the very old and the new gives it a gracious charm. During the Spanish occupation of what is now

Florida, St. Augustine was an important fortress looking out on the Atlantic Ocean. Modern St. Augustine is a favorite of tourists, drawn by near-perfect weather, one of the best beaches on the coast, and the restored ruins of Castillo De San Marcos, whose rugged battlements once withstood enemies from the sea.

As the civil rights bill moved into the Senate arena in Washington, St. Augustine played an important role in emphasizing the appeal for open public accommodations in America.

In the year 1964, St. Augustine observed its four hundredth birthday, and a celebration was in order. Plans were made well in advance, and a national promotion campaign was mounted to entice the maximum number of tourists and history buffs. The planned celebration also attracted some unwanted attention.

Although one out of four residents of St. Augustine (1964 population 16,000) was black, there was no black involvement in the celebration activities. And if black tourists came to town, white-only lodging places would not admit them. The town leadership actually did not appear aware of the implications. The blacks seemed to live "happily" to themselves in their part of town; they were far removed from the civil rights furor elsewhere in the country; and they provided a plentiful and cheap source of labor to prepare St. Augustine for its big birthday.

There was an active, but small, black organization in town, informally affiliated with Martin Luther King's Southern Christian Leadership Conference, but it was very low-keyed. Some steps had been taken voluntarily by the community that appeared to fully satisfy local black residents: schools were desegregated without a court order, and Mayor Joe Shelley quietly desegregated facilities in municipal offices when he was elected two years before. Some eating places were integrated without fuss or fanfare. But public lodging was not desegregated.

Despite this show of racial progress, King moved almost his entire organization into St. Augustine for what he called a "point of no return" confrontation. City fathers stubbornly balked at what they considered a forced imposition. And so the die was cast for St. Augustine to become, almost overnight, a crisis spot in the campaign to win total integration of public facilities in the nation.

Thus did this quiet little city become a showcase for those in Congress pushing for a new civil rights act with a public accommodations section opening every motel and hotel in the country to anyone, regardless of race. For Martin Luther King, Jr., St. Augustine was a perfect focal point.

As was the custom of civil rights activists, it was announced that they had been "invited," but the invitation came from a small group within the black population. Most local blacks at first deplored, ignored, or were openly angered at this intrusion of controversy when gradualism appeared to be working.

As a daily and nightly observer of all these incidents, I sometimes had mental flashbacks to the days of my childhood and the vigorous game of cowboys and Indians, wherein one day the cowboys prevailed and the next day the Indians, all in not-so-innocent fun. In the early days of the St. Augustine campaign, grownup boys played their games and collected their points without meaning to hurt anyone. But the mood changed as the black demonstrators began bearing down on the emphasis they were trying to get across to the white establishment.

The Monson Motor Lodge in St. Augustine was doing a thriving tourist business. Strategically situated at the main entrance to the old city, its swimming pool and restaurant in plain view of travelers on U.S. Highway A1A, the lodge stood to gain perhaps more than any other merchant from the big birthday party. The lodge was strictly segregated. One of the managers explained that "it's not because we care whether niggers stay here but we'd go out of business the first time we let one in." King was adept at spotting such chinks in the walls of segregation.

Upon his arrival in quiet, apparently peaceful, drowsy St. Augustine, King's people brought out the opponents of integration in short order, and, for a time, plans for the anniversary were all but obliterated. The white segregation element was just beneath the veneer and glitter of the tourist town, and it was determined to thwart the black effort.

Sheriff L.O. Davis, with his force of one hundred deputies, had all he could do to maintain a semblance of order. Every day some new incident added to the pressure: the time that blacks marched into town from one direction and a force of whites marched toward the same spot from another direction, only to be diverted at the last moment; the day there was a wade-in at the beach, the town's pristine strip of all-white sand.

Meet Hostead (Hoss) Manucy. He is white, thirtyish at that time, a paunchy ex-deputy sheriff. He drove a beat-up old sedan equipped with wide tires for getting around on beach sand. Inside was two-way radio equipment that turned his rattletrap into an effective communications unit. Hoss Manucy, leader of the Ancient City Hunting Club, was one of the self-appointed guardians of white supremacy in St. Augustine. He gave the alert by radio that two young blacks were on their way to the beach. Within minutes he was joined by companions.

A group of about fifty segregationists clashes with civil rights demonstrators in the Atlantic surf of a St. Augustine beach on June 6, 1964. The violence occurred when the demonstrators made a second attempt that day to use the normally all-white beach. Photo: © Bettmann-Corbis

Into the surf went the blacks, and into the surf after them came the whites. After some thrashing around and a few duckings, both sides came out, each claiming victory.

It went on like that for several days, playacting on a serious theme, until a federal court injunction ordered Manucy to leave blacks alone. Thereafter, he lived a subdued life.

On another occasion, King and a small party of his people, having given ample notice to reporters, walked up to the front door of the Monson Motor Lodge. The manager blocked the entrance. "I would like to have a room," King said, as though he did that sort of thing regularly in St. Augustine. The poor manager really didn't care whether King had a room. He simply feared his place would go out of business if King were admitted. He turned the black man away. A Justice Department attorney in the little crowd recorded the event.

This was the sort of point-making King practiced all the time, as though he followed a checklist of items of public accommodations being considered by the Congress.

One day the swimming pool at the lodge became the center of attention. This was another of those crumbling bastions of segregation that the white opponents of integration were determined to preserve at all costs.

After days of trying, two young blacks managed to slip through the ring of whites guarding the pool and plunged in. Two whites leaped in to pull them out while the manager quickly grabbed a large plastic jug of fluid and raced around the water's edge, pouring the stuff into the pool. This, of course, was caught on the cameras of a dozen news and television cameramen, and word spread around the country that the whites had tried to poison the black swimmers. Anti-climactically, the fluid was finally identified as laundry bleach that added only a tiny bit to the amount of chlorine already in the water.

One of the most popular tourist spots in downtown St. Augustine is what local literature called an old slave market. Here, the black drivers of horse-drawn carriages picked up their white fares and had themselves photographed with the visitors. The site, a small covered pavilion, became the symbolic goal of the St. Augustine demonstrators. Night after night, black marchers, sometimes joined by a few white "outside agitators," formed ranks in the black part of town and marched in double file toward the slave market. Andrew Young, later to become a member of Congress from Georgia, United Nations ambassador, and mayor of Atlanta, often led the procession.

With equal regularity, the white opposition tried to break the singing ranks of blacks, smashing into the marchers with sweating white bodies and with more solid objects: tire tools, lengths of chain, and heavy staves. It was an act, a game that had nothing to do with the goal of desegregating Monson Motor Lodge. Yet, it was this nightly game, and not events at the lodge, that built up the tempers in St. Augustine.

One morning, I left the noisy slave market park and entered the quiet sanctuary of Christ Episcopal Church across the street. There, I talked with one of the clergy who said the members were very worried about the violence being visited on the peaceful city. His major concern, however, was that a rock might be thrown through the magnificent stained glass window facing the slave market.

The night marches were finally banned by local court order on grounds they were "for the sole purpose of creating disorder or possible violence." But Federal District Judge Bryan Simpson overturned that decision, prohibiting interference with the black marchers. Having no stomach for a federal jail on contempt charges, the whites were successfully discouraged from continuing the marching game. Then they tried one final ploy before giving up altogether.

Al Kuettner interviews militant segregationist J.B. Stoner (right), chairman of the National States Rights Party. Stoner was convicted in 1980 of conspiracy in the 1958 bombing of the Bethel Baptist Church in Birmingham. He died in 2005. Photo: © Joseph M. Chapman

If the federal judge said the blacks could march into the white part of town, then the whites could march into the black part of town, an area southeast of the slave market. So they planned a countermarch, and it was organized by J.B. Stoner, a militant segregationist from Atlanta.

Bear in mind, these were grown men, mostly in their twenties, thirties, and forties: family men, working men, men coming out for sport at night, like going to a ball game. They planned their sortie into black St. Augustine with all the gravity of a military engagement. Then came the appointed night. News of the impending march had spread for days, so there were no surprise elements. Go in, come out—that was their only tactic. A crowd of white marchers, police, and reporters gathered for the adventure.

The black section of St. Augustine was so unprepossessing it did not even have a name. I never heard it called "Nigger Town," the standard label in many Southern cities. Most white people, including a number of the night marchers, knew little or nothing about the area. White matrons who drove out there and honked maids from their houses knew how it looked on the outside, but they never let themselves get closer to the community than the curb.

The main street of the black community was lined with one- and two-story buildings, much like an old western cow town. The street was only dimly lighted. It was to this area, a twenty-minute march from the slave market, that the white demonstrators headed. The march stepped off raggedly without signal. State troopers at the head of the column moved first. The place was swarming with police, spaced at intervals along the marching column, and at intersections. They were there to prevent violence when the whites and blacks confronted each other in the near darkness.

The presence of so many police, an occasional message arriving from some officer up the line, and the general atmosphere of mystery about what lay ahead produced its special kind of tension among the whites. Their expletive-punctuated bragging of a few days' past was gone, and talk was subdued. Spirits improved a bit with the march under way, but sagged again as the front of the column maneuvered a short dogleg to the right, then to the left, and entered the street of their destination. Not a sound was heard except for the shuffling of feet. It was impossible at first to see. Very dimly, then, as I passed beneath it, I noted the lettering of a large banner that stretched across the street entrance. It read: "WELCOME."

Pushed along by those behind, the column of marchers moved further into the street. As my eyes became accustomed to the darkness, I could make out dimly the forms of people lining one side of the street, silently watching the procession from storefront shadows. Soon, the street was filled with the white marchers, and with police and reporters. As though by some internal signal, the blacks now came to life. They stepped forward, and with one voice began singing the old spiritual adopted as Martin Luther King's civil rights hymn: "We shall overcome . . . some sweet day."

The whites were dumbfounded, confused, and, I suspect, humiliated by the experience. After milling around for a few moments, they broke ranks and left hurriedly.

An unreported (until now) meeting of the black and white leadership in St. Augustine was finally held. Some of the participants had never spoken to, or been near, those of the other race in St. Augustine. They came from opposite ends of town after assurances that their session would be in secret.

Words, halting at first, provided exposure for the grievances on one side and problems with those grievances on the other side. The wife of a black participant said, "The air was like a furnace coming out of that room. All I knew to do was turn a big fan on them."

Within a few days, the St. Augustine demonstrations ended without formal agreement. The whites were glad for the return of normalcy; blacks felt they had made another strong point in their insistence on full rights to public facilities. In Washington, Congress noted the points made—and that was the whole purpose of St. Augustine.

President Johnson shakes hands with civil rights leader Martin Luther King, Jr., and hands him a pen after signing the Civil Rights Act on July 2, 1964. Photo: © Bettmann-Corbis

CHAPTER **11**

1964–Civil Rights Act Passes

"Let us close the springs of racial poison."

—President Johnson

"Those who deny freedom to others deserve it not for themselves, and under a just God, cannot long retain it."

—Abraham Lincoln

President Johnson knew the administration still had a fight ahead to obtain Senate approval of the House-passed civil rights bill. If adopted in its present form, the measure would set aside old customs affecting almost all Americans and establish practices that would be applicable to all citizens under authority of law.

Johnson asked Minnesota Senator Hubert H. Humphrey to manage the showdown in the Senate for the administration side. Humphrey, the majority whip, was shrewd and battle-wise in Senate fights, yet persuasive, popular with colleagues, and with a sense of humor as well as charm. For the president, Humphrey turned out to be an ideal choice.

LBJ had his own brand of humor. He loved Humphrey, the "Happy Warrior," and had deep respect for the man's ability to sway Congress. But those he loved the best, Johnson kidded the most. So, in asking him to take on this most difficult task of his legislative career, the president told him he was doing it to give him a chance, to see if he really had the ability to get things done.

Advocates of passage of the civil rights bill faced formidable opposition. For one thing, there was the Senate's cherished right to have unlimited debate, thus being able to talk legislation to death by filibuster. Never in history had the Senate mustered the required two-thirds vote to shut off debate on a civil rights bill. Furthermore, the opposition was led by Southern

Democrats who had dominated Senate leadership for many years. The chairman of the Judiciary Committee to which such legislation as civil rights ordinarily was sent was Senator James O. Eastland of Mississippi, one of the most dedicated proponents of racial segregation.

In a Senate speech February 17, 1964, Senator Mike Mansfield, the Montana Democrat and Senate majority leader, professed not to possess any "suave parliamentary tactics" by which to bring legislation to a vote. "But," he said, "even if there were parliamentary tricks or tactics, Mr. President, the Majority Leader would not be inclined to employ them. I can think of nothing better designed to bring this institution into public disrepute and derision than a test of this profound and tragic issue by an exercise in parliamentary pyrotechnics."

Nine days later, the Senate voted 74-37 to place HR 7152, the civil rights bill, directly on the Senate calendar for floor debate, thus bypassing the Southern-dominated Judiciary Committee.

Undismayed by this early setback, the Southern strategy began to appear on the morning of March 9 on a motion by Senator Mansfield to take up the civil rights bill for consideration. Under a Senate rule, such a motion cannot be debated if it is made during the so-called "morning hour" which ends at 2 p.m. In this instance, Georgia Senator Richard B. Russell, leader of the bill's opposition, forced Mansfield by parliamentary maneuver to delay his motion until after 2 p.m. This trick subjected the motion to unlimited debate, and the first filibuster of the bill's trip through the Senate began.

After seventeen days of these delaying tactics, Mansfield's motion to get started on the bill itself was brought to a Senate vote. It passed 67-17 with just about every member in favor except the Southern bloc. "We lost a skirmish, now we begin to fight the war," Russell commented.

Democratic and Republican "Captains of the Bill" began holding nightly meetings to discuss and develop strategy. Twice a week civil rights groups were invited into the meetings to listen. Dr. Martin Luther King, Jr., came to town and held a news conference in the Capitol. He said that civil rights demonstrations would continue even if the bill under debate passed, because enforcement and compliance would have to be tested.

Formal debate on HR 7152 was opened by Senator Humphrey who said, in urging passage, that "our Union will remain profoundly imperfect" so long as racial justice and freedom are not a reality.

There were many speeches made in the Senate for and against this new "moral code of behavior," as advocates labeled it, but none more to the point than that delivered by Senator Humphrey in opening the Senate debate.

"Mr. President," Humphrey said on March 26, 1964, "Today is the ninety-fourth anniversary of the ratification of the Fifteenth Amendment . . . Like the Gettysburg Address, it is of continuing historic significance and highly important. It reads as follows: 'Section 1. The right of citizens of the United States to vote shall not be denied or abridged by the United States or by any state on account of race, color, or previous condition of servitude. Section 2. The Congress shall have power to enforce this article by appropriate legislation.'"

Humphrey reminded members that this basic right to vote was denied to millions of Americans on account of race, leaving many blacks "taxed without representation" because they were not allowed to vote. He cited less than 7 percent of eligible blacks registered in Mississippi compared to 70 percent of the white adult population. Then he noted it had been argued that "Negroes are really not very interested in voting," but that in one Southern state, Florida, a higher percentage of blacks voted than whites.

Humphrey hit hard at "double standards" of voter qualification where white voters were routinely approved and blacks routinely rejected, often for failure to pass complicated tests. He cited one of the many Alabama tests that blacks had complained about. "In one county the principal of a local Negro school was turned away on five successive visits to the voting office. Finally on the sixth visit he was permitted to fill out the forms and take the Constitutional interpretation test. He was asked to interpret a section of the state constitution that was so complex it had given difficulty to the State Supreme Court." Humphrey saved his heaviest oratory for the controversial public accommodations section of the bill.

"It is difficult for most of us to fully comprehend the monstrous humiliations and inconveniences that racial discrimination imposes on our Negro fellow citizens," he said. "If a white man is thirsty on a hot day, he goes to the nearest soda fountain . . . But for a Negro the picture is different. Trying to get a glass of iced tea at a lunch counter may result in insult and abuse . . . He can never count on using a restroom, on getting a decent place to stay, on buying a good meal."

The senator then referred to two guidebooks in his possession, one for white travelers with pets, the other for blacks without pets. "It is heartbreaking to compare these two guidebooks, the one for families with dogs, and the other for Negroes," Humphrey said. "In Augusta, Georgia, for example, there are five hotels and motels that will take dogs, and only one where a Negro can go with confidence. In Columbus, Georgia, there are six places for dogs, and none for Negroes. In Charleston, South Carolina, there are ten places where a dog can stay, and none for a Negro." He suggested that whites would be raising their voices "above the babel of self-righteousness" just as blacks were doing if the situation were reversed.

Humphrey denied that most Southern businesses opposed the public accommodations proposal on racial grounds, but "are balked" by community pressure or fear of losing trade.

"We must hasten the day when Negro families and children can travel on every bit of this land without the fear that they will be refused a place of rest because of the accident of birth. We must insure to the same family that it can enter a restaurant in its own community as the equal of every other family there. We must make certain that every door in our public places of refinement and culture is open to men (and women) with black skin as well as white. In sum, we must put an end to the shabby treatment of the Negro in public places which demeans him and debases the value of his American citizenship."

The Humphrey forces were face to face with perhaps the strongest pro-segregation Southern opposition in history—orators, cloakroom traders, masters of maneuver. One of the most effective was the veteran Georgia Democrat, Senator Richard B. Russell. In a Senate speech on June 10, Russell said: "Equal rights in this land of ours means that each citizen has an equal opportunity to acquire property through honest means, that once that property has been acquired, he has a right to exercise dominion over it. Under our system, many Negroes have accumulated great amounts of property. It is not equality to pass laws that give any group, whoever they may be, the right to violate the property rights of another that are guaranteed by the Constitution."

On another occasion, Russell complained that the civil rights bill had been "stripped of any pretense, and stands as a purely sectional bill." He said amendments had insured that states outside the South would be exempt from "its most punitive provisions."

Russell also objected strongly to the clergy's role in making a great moral issue out of what the Georgia senator contended was purely a political issue. "There were many ministers who, having failed completely in their effort to establish good will and brotherhood from the pulpit, turned from the pulpit to the powers of the federal government to coerce the people into accepting their views under threat of dire punishment," Russell said.

Both sides geared up for a debate which Mansfield acknowledged "could go on for months." The Southern bloc organized its battle plan, dividing into three filibuster platoons under Democratic Senators Allen J. Ellender of Louisiana, John Stennis of Mississippi, and Lister Hill of Alabama. Each group had six members, except for Hill's team that also contained Senator John Tower of Texas, the only Republican in the nineteen-member Southern bloc.

The strategy was that, while one team held the Senate floor, the others could be absent from the chamber. The Southerners could demand a roll call at will, forcing the opposition to establish a quick alert system to round up members for these calls. At times, the system broke down.

The South demanded one quorum call during a dinner hour, requiring a wait of sixty-three minutes while senators were disturbed at their tables and hustled into the chamber to answer their presence.

The filibuster droned on for almost two months, until finally on the morning of June 10, the Senate voted 71-29 to shut off the Southern delaying tactics. The cloture vote, requiring a two-thirds majority, passed with only four votes to spare.

By the time the Senate debate ended, 560 amendments had been offered, most of them by the South. Only ten were accepted for consideration, although Russell warned that Southerners would insist on calling up all they had proposed. "We are confronted here not only with the spirit of the mob, but of the lynch mob," he said. "There is no reason to expect any fairness."

It was now obvious that the opposition to a civil rights law had lost the battle. The voices of debate were soon stilled, shut off like turning a water tap. On June 19 the Senate passed the civil rights bill by a vote of 73-27, in essentially the same form as the bill that had come over from the House. The few amendments requiring House concurrence were hurried over to that chamber which cleared the Senate-approved bill on July 2 by a roll call vote of 289-126. As the measure went down to the final moments, three House members switched from earlier approval to disapproval, and three others switched their votes from No to Yes.

One of those who changed to approving the legislation was Representative Charles L. Weltner, Democrat of Georgia, who represented the city of Atlanta. In a statement before casting his vote, Weltner said that Southerners had a choice.

"Change, swift and certain, is upon us, and we in the South face some difficult decisions. We can offer resistance and defiance, with their harvest of strife and tumult. We can suffer continued demonstrations, with their wake of violence and disorder. Or we can acknowledge this measure as the law of the land. We can accept the verdict of the nation," he said.

"Already, the responsible elements of my community are counseling this latter course, and most assuredly moderation, tranquility, and orderly processes combined as a cause greater than mere conformity . . . I will add my voice to those who seek reasoned and conciliatory adjustment to a new reality. Finally, I would urge that we at home now move on to the unfinished task of building a new South. We must not remain forever bound to another lost cause."

In its final form the new law had these major provisions:

Voting Rights–The same standards must be applied to all in qualifying to vote in federal elections (for president, vice president, presidential electors, Senate and House). If literacy tests are used they must be given to all or none, and in writing. A sixth grade education is a general guide for voter qualification. Appeal mechanism is provided through the office of Attorney General.

Public Accommodations–All persons shall be entitled to full and equal enjoyment of goods, services, facilities, privileges, advantages, and accommodations "without discrimination or segregation on the ground of race, color, religion, or national origin." Places of public accommodation include inns, hotels, motels or other facilities with more than five rooms for hire that provide lodging to transient guests; public eating places, motion picture houses, theaters, concert halls, sports arenas, or other public places of entertainment.

It is discrimination if segregation is supported by state law, custom or usage. The Act provides for appeal mechanism with U. S. liable for attorney fees. Attorney General may bring civil action before three-judge federal court, and if he fails to act, the chief judge of the District shall act.

Desegregation of Public Facilities–Anyone claiming to be discriminated against in a public facility on account of race, color, religion, or national origin may ask the Attorney General to initiate civil court action.

Desegregation of Public Education–Desegregation means assignment of students to public schools without regard to race, color, religion, or national origin, but desegregation "shall not mean the assignment of students to public schools in order to overcome racial imbalance." The Act provides for Commissioner of Education to assist school boards in implementing desegregation, and provides for training institutes to help school personnel learn to deal with problems of desegregation (federal government pays for training on request). Attorney General shall file suit in federal court on accepted complaint that law is not being obeyed.

Commission on Civil Rights–Act sets up an investigative body to hold hearings, study and collect information, serve as clearinghouse for information, investigate allegations.

Non-Discrimination in Federally Assisted Programs–No person in U.S. on grounds of race, color, religion, or national origin shall be excluded under any program receiving federal financial assistance.

Equal Employment Opportunity–With some exemptions it is unlawful to discriminate against hiring or retaining employees on basis of race, color, religion, or national origin in order to classify employees in a discriminatory way. It is unlawful for a labor organization to discriminate, unlawful to apply different standards of compensation, unlawful to advertise for employment indicating a preference based on race, color, religion, or national origin. Act creates an Equal Employment Opportunity Commission to hear and refer to Attorney General complaints. Commission has wide investigative authority.

Registration and Voting Statistics–Act provides for collection of voting statistics such as persons voting by race, color, and national origin, extent to which they are registered to vote and have voted in statewide primaries or general elections in which members of the House of Representatives were elected since January 1, 1960. Census shall be used to obtain information. Act expressly provides that no one is required to give such information and they must be advised of their right to refuse.

Establishment of Community Relations Service–Provides assistance to communities and individuals on civil rights compliance and disputes. (Service later disbanded under a provision of Civil Rights Act that permits the step when Service is deemed no longer needed.)

Within hours of final passage, President Johnson assembled congressional and civil rights leaders, and several Cabinet members and foreign ambassadors, in the East Room of the White House. At 6:45 p.m. on national television, he signed the 1964 Civil Rights Act.

The president asked all Americans "to join in this effort to bring justice and hope to all our people—and peace to our land. Let us close the springs of racial poison."

John Lewis (light coat, center) attempts to ward off the blow as a state trooper swings his club at Lewis' head during the March 7, 1965, attempted march from Selma to Montgomery. Lewis suffered a concussion and was hospitalized. Photo: © Bettmann-Corbis

CHAPTER 12

1964–The Selma Story, Part 1

"Let's walk to Montgomery."

—A young volunteer

"You often say, 'I would give, but only to the deserving.' The trees in your orchard say not so, nor the flocks in your pasture. They give that they may live, for to withhold is to perish."

—The Prophet, Kahlil Gibran

The ink was hardly dry on the 1964 Civil Rights Act, with its voting, public accommodations, and education provisions, before still another important measure was headed for debate in 1965. Again, it concentrated on voting rights.

It is fair to ask why all this was necessary. Why was not the voting rights issue covered thoroughly in the 1964 legislation, passed after such grueling argument? The answer is that the Congress is a body of deliberative compromise; managers of the 1964 legislation got all they could, and really much more than they expected.

The 1964 Act barred unequal application of voting registration requirements, prohibited denial of the right to vote because of minor omissions on application records, required that all literacy tests be administered in writing, and made a sixth-grade education a presumption of literacy. But the legislation was limited to federal elections—for president, vice president, congressional representatives, and senators.

As blacks in the South sought to register in large numbers under the Act, it soon became obvious that the 1964 law did not go far enough for them. Election procedures traditionally were under control of local communities, counties, and states. Some places chose to ignore the 1964 law, falling back on local rules of registration. One of those places was Selma, Alabama.

In all the records of the mid-twentieth century racial revolution, Selma must ever stand out to blacks as a symbol of struggle against an entrenched adversary. They were determined to win full equality in the right to vote—from the presidency to the least of local officials. Selma was the battleground.

This central Alabama town lies fifty miles west of the state capital at Montgomery, eighty-four miles southeast of the state university at Tuscaloosa, and in that year many, many miles from the reality of what was happening in the South.

All around, there was evidence of change: the state universities in Alabama and next door in Mississippi had been integrated, albeit only with the use of federal enforcement; Birmingham, 110 miles to the north, had come to terms with blacks on the desegregation of shopping and eating facilities; Montgomery had gone through a 381-day boycott that ended in desegregation of buses; Central High School in Little Rock, Arkansas, was open to black students following a state standoff that was ended by the arrival of federalized troops; and Congress had passed a sweeping new civil rights act that clearly pointed the way to a new system of racial tolerance. Yet, at the end of 1964, it was as though Selma was an invisibly walled city, separated from its neighbors by a moat of oblivion, protecting its past in seeming peace and harmony.

Dallas County, where Selma is the county seat, had more blacks than whites, but with only 275 black registered voters in 1965 to 9,800 white registrants. Voter registration books were open only two days a month, and no more than thirty blacks were allowed to register in a day. The Justice Department filed suit in 1965 to remove a new Alabama voter registration test for blacks that contained four questions on government, four on the Constitution, and a section that required recall of portions of the Constitution. With more than one hundred variations of the test, it was virtually impossible to study for the exam. Whites were passed routinely after only a few elementary questions.

Martin Luther King, Jr., and a black group called the Selma Improvement Association took up the voter registration fight in January 1965. The goal was to break the voting barrier at the Dallas County courthouse and to demonstrate the plight of Selma blacks to the White House and to Congress.

At that time, Dallas County was mostly rural. In its population of 15,800, blacks represented 80.7 percent. The white social and religious leadership held sway, appearing on the surface to genuinely feel that they were beginning to comply with the new civil rights act; to them King, his outsiders, and the news media were wholly responsible for the racial troubles.

At first, there was not much excitement or concern in the white community about the brash blacks who vowed to "stir up things" in their town. They did not think anything would come of the boastful effort. They would stay awhile, yell and sing, collect all the money they could from "our decent, law-abiding Negroes," and go their way to some other town. Downtown, all was quiet. The Dallas County courthouse was running routine business in the same way many another county courthouse was operated: taxes, wills, marriage licenses, the courtroom upstairs that was always a center of interest on court days, like a new movie in town—and the voter registration office. Everything was neatly segregated the way it had always been, and none of the locals thought it was going to change.

The Improvement Association set up headquarters at Brown's Chapel, a black Methodist A.M.E. church that was typical of so many used as staging areas during a civil rights campaign. Night after night the church resounded to hymns, speeches, and exhortations as the effort began to attract crowds and money. The churches seemed pleased to have the civil rights groups using their buildings, but the heavy use of electricity and winter heat finally caused some to ask politely for a little financial contribution to pay the bills.

On January 3, 1965, Martin Luther King, Jr., opened the Selma drive at Brown's Chapel with these words: "We must be willing to go to jail by the thousands. We are not asking—we are demanding the ballot."

Sixteen days later, King was attacked in the lobby of the Albert Hotel when he put hotel registration for blacks to the local test. He was turned down. King, in his first desegregation drive since winning the Nobel Peace Prize, was not seriously hurt by the white man, Jimmy George Robinson, who slugged him in the face. Robinson, an organizer for the National States Rights Party in Dallas, Texas, was hauled out of the lobby by local police and jailed.

Speaking of King's attempt to register for a room, Charles Keys, an Anniston, Alabama, segregationist who witnessed the episode, told a small group: "If twenty-two years ago King had done what he did today, he would have been strung to a tree. He couldn't have raped the city of Selma the way he did today." Characteristically, King said he held "no malice" toward Robinson, calling him "a symbol of the sickness in our society . . . I have nothing but pity and compassion for this man."

In those early January days of the Selma drive, the voter registration effort seemed at first to be encountering success. On one day about three hundred blacks were admitted to the courthouse where the registration office was located. And three restaurants in town served blacks without complaint. But these surface gains soon were discounted by facts. Although no blacks were barred from the courthouse at the outset of the campaign, no one was actually able to register.

King told reporters that blacks, after going in the front door of the courthouse, were given numbers, sent out the back door, and "herded into an alley like animals" to wait for their numbers to be called—which never happened. King promised to return to the courthouse until all who wanted to do so were registered.

Black Alabama citizens were still faced with complicated voting tests at the time of the Selma campaign. King argued that the ability to write name and address should be ample qualification for voting everywhere. "The day must come when the literacy test must be done away with altogether," he said. "And if local registration bogs down, we feel there should be federal registration"—a step that would permit a turned-down applicant to "go right down to the United States Post Office and register."

Meanwhile, the nightly rallies at Brown's Chapel and other black churches continued. On one occasion, at the First Baptist Church where six hundred blacks were gathered to hear Dr. King, George Lincoln Rockwell, head of the American Nazi Party, arrived for the rally. He claimed King had invited him, but the civil rights leader had not yet arrived. Police Commissioner Wilson Baker, who kept regular attendance on these events, asked a black leader at the church if Rockwell had been invited. "I'm sure we don't want him," Baker was told. Rockwell refused to leave and said he would have to be arrested. "OK, you're under arrest," Baker told him, and off to jail he went.

The nightly collection to fuel the civil rights movement was always a big part of every meeting. There is no way of knowing how many poor black people in the South fed the movement with their last pennies. During a meeting one night at some now-forgotten church, I wandered into a back room looking for a telephone. The collection had just been taken, and the money had been brought to the room, vacant and unguarded. I saw about six large baskets on the table, each of them overflowing with bills. It was always a mystery as to who kept the accounts. But the movement had its goals, stated its needs, and repeatedly passed the baskets.

Often, King left a place like Selma for a midnight flight to some fund-raising rally in the East or West. He never received a speeding ticket in those days, although he would be driven at racetrack speeds to make flights. Troopers were always glad to see him go, so long as he was leaving the state. He logged two hundred fifty thousand air miles in 1964 alone.

Much speculation was spread that King was getting rich personally off the blacks he enlisted. I know of no evidence to substantiate the stories. King's salary was one dollar per year plus expenses. The Kings always lived in modest homes and most of the time their children attended public schools. King contributed the $54,600 he received as winner of the Nobel Peace Prize to the civil rights movement. Following his death, his widow, Coretta, had to conduct a campaign privately to raise funds for her husband's memorial.

The month of January 1965 in Selma was wet and cold. Sylvan Street outside Brown's Chapel was muddy and miserable. This was the bivouac area of several hundred civil rights activists, most of them black, but with some white sympathizers; they were determined to hold out until blacks were freely allowed to register to vote in local elections.

Their leaders schooled them meanwhile in Martin Luther King's philosophy of nonviolence. Bald, olive-skinned Reverend James Bevel, one of King's most intense revolutionaries, told a crowd at Brown's Chapel: "Some people have a hard time understanding nonviolence. They try to spread the teachings of Jesus by using Caesar's methods."

I suppose the situation in Selma might be likened to getting a splinter under a fingernail, worrisome but bearable; finally turning mean and painful. This was a campaign that built up gradually, from a nuisance to the white establishment to a full-blown public crisis. Reaching downtown, just eight blocks from their church, became a symbolic goal of the blacks. At first, sheriff's deputies at the county courthouse simply turned back black voter applicants with a few sharp words. As the crowds increased, authority became more severe, and blacks were jailed or chased away from the courthouse.

After a few weeks of these confrontations, white city police set up a single line across Sylvan Street one hundred yards from Brown's Chapel. Their job was to contain the blacks. Don't let them get to the courthouse. Practically, it was a useless maneuver; symbolically, it worked for a while. It was simple to walk around the police lines and through the George Washington Carver housing project across the street—but no one did. That would not have been part of the game. A small delegation would walk from the church to the line and ask to pass. Permission denied. Back to the church. More songs, more speeches. Back to the line. "We love everybody," they sang. Blacks loved symbols, for they broke the boredom of their lives—and now the whites were cooperating by bringing one of their own inventions to rain-soaked Sylvan Street.

And it rained, and rained. It was the wet and cold of late February and early March that I remember most about the Selma experience. Whether for or against these people in the street, they had to get some credit for a lot of spunk. I was one of the fortunate. A black family in the housing project with a front row seat onto the demonstrations at first permitted me to use their telephone—my lifeline to the outside world—but soon let me have the run of their apartment. There was not much sleep to be had in those days and nights on Sylvan Street, but drying out and an occasional rest with a cup of hot coffee meant everything.

It was here that I found blacks willing to risk censure by taking me in—response from the heart to basic human needs, where color consciousness disappeared. This has to be my belated note of gratitude for I never learned their names. And they never said whether they believed in or deplored what was happening. One woman kept saying, "Lord, I pray nobody gets hurt."

The Edmundite Fathers and Brothers, a group of white Roman Catholic priests and laymen who operated a mission and hospital for the Selma community, endorsed the voting drive. Their full-page advertisement appeared in the Selma Times Journal: "America is fortunate that the Negro leadership is, on the whole, temperate and dedicated to American ideals. It is when their so-obviously just claims are ignored, their needs completely unattended, their just demands refused; it is when local-courts are closed to them because no protective laws apply, that the streets become their only means of protest. We know from personal experience of the truth of the Negro claims of injustice and the evil effects of discrimination on his mind, body and soul. Like good Selma citizens, we grieve at the crisis within our city. But we think that those who are concerned about the image of Selma should take heart. The real image of any city trying to find solutions to the complex problems of racial discrimination will shine forth in the honest efforts of its citizens to work together for justice. This we are convinced will be Selma's lasting image."

For days and nights, the chief point of contest between the blacks and whites was that thin police line in the street, and whether it would be removed. After awhile, the demonstrators formed their own line facing the white officers, and there they did their standoff, ten feet apart. A number of tense confrontations at this symbolic barricade, promptly labeled Selma's "Maginot Line," ranged from a few shouters to crowds of more than one thousand.

Federal agents (easily identifiable in their neat suits) and local officers looked on, as did journalists from most of the major papers, agencies, and networks. So did observers of the new Federal Community Relations Service, established by the 1964 Civil Rights Act to monitor progress of compliance. Late one rainy night LeRoy Collins, the former governor of Florida who had been chosen by the president as first director of the agency, walked across the line on an inspection tour. The arrival of such a high-level official from Washington, or some new convert from the outside world, always sent a wave of optimism through the movement.

The demonstrators could have gone inside the church where it was warm and dry; but few ever did, except to eat at a soup kitchen in the basement. They sat or lay in the rain, protected by tents, tarpaulins, newspapers, cardboard boxes, anything they could find. Some just took it wet, huddled around smoky campfires. Spontaneously, songs would break out among the soaked congregation.

Men, women, and children were there in the street, side by side, and the stories inevitably spread that the Selma Movement was one big sex orgy under those shelters. With that large a mixed crowd, anywhere, sex often becomes a factor. But orgy? Not in Selma. One reporter started that story, based on second- and third-hand rumors he never checked out. The lurid account gave him a one-day "beat" over all other reporters on the Selma scene and forced us off the main story to run down the rumors. Much of our time was wasted in that manner.

And so the days of Selma grew into weeks. One day, without public explanation, the police barricade at the church was removed. Now came the larger challenge: to actually get people's names on the voter registration list. Downtown, there was steady harassment of the blacks and the "outsider" whites who supported them.

With the shift of the demonstrations from Sylvan Street to the courthouse, the informality of the opposition disappeared and at times turned ugly and deadly. The out-of-state white sympathizers were held in utter contempt by the local white segregationists. One was the Reverend James Reeb of New York City. On March 12 in downtown Selma, two blocks from the courthouse, Reeb and some friends were accosted as they emerged from a black restaurant. Reeb was fatally beaten. Three white businessmen were arrested, tried, and acquitted.

In nearby Marion, Alabama, about the same time, Jimmie Lee Jackson, a young black, was killed by a white state trooper. Witnesses claimed Jackson was trying to shield his mother from a beating during a racial demonstration in Marion that was part of King's central Alabama voter registration drive in the Selma area. Jackson was brought to a Selma hospital where he died. The officer was cleared by a grand jury.

The violence seemed to intensify rather than deter the black campaigners. Their strategy was simple. They refused to enter the courthouse through the side door as ordered; they stood in line rain or shine to register; they returned the next day, and the next, to insist on the right to vote; and they accepted arrest.

Martin Luther King, Jr., was one of more than 3,300 blacks jailed during the long voter registration drive in Selma and its environs. In a single day, King and 770 other blacks, including 500 school children who had skipped classes, were arrested while picketing the Dallas County courthouse. School buses were used to haul children to a makeshift enclosure. A militant Sheriff James C. Clark supervised the arrests.

Annie Lee Cooper, fifty-three at the time, a black woman in the voting effort, became enraged and struck the sheriff—an unforgivable sin. She was clubbed to the ground by Clark and two deputies. Newspapers and news networks featured a photograph of Mrs. Cooper, on her back with arms held spread-eagled by two officers while a third had his club raised in a strike position.

The people of Selma did not know how to handle this new and, to them, frightening development. To watch the scenes from Birmingham and other flash points on television was one thing; they thought it was terrible, but a safe distance away. Here, it was right in their front yard. The solution chosen by most whites was to ignore the whole thing. Let the sheriff handle the problem; it was his courthouse; he was paid to keep order there. And so most stayed away from the courthouse scene, did not see the daily lines of blacks waiting to register, or the loads of school children swelling the demonstration. Most of the people of Selma thus failed to witness this episode in the collapse of segregation in their pretty little town.

Most of the arrests were the revolving-door type—in and out of jail, sometimes within an hour. It was almost impossible for us to keep a head count on arrests because many of the enthusiastic youngsters would be jailed and released in the morning, be back in jail in the afternoon, and occasionally, be in again that night. The negotiating price for many a racial settlement—Selma's included—was the dismissal of all police charges or school disciplinary action against the demonstrators.

Just before his arrest, King told a rally at Brown's Chapel: "If Negroes could vote, there would be no Jim Clarks, there would be no oppressive poverty directed against Negroes. Our children would not be crippled by segregated schools, and the whole community might live together in harmony. This is our intention: to declare war on the evils of demagoguery. The entire community will join in this protest, and we will not relent until there is change in the voting process and the establishment of democracy."

Selma's rotund public safety director, Wilson Baker, kept order wherever his men had jurisdiction. But the courthouse was the territory of Sheriff Clark, a county officer. Baker stood by and watched helplessly, listening to Clark tongue-lash blacks with his military-like orders: "You people must stay four feet apart; you must not block the sidewalk." Must . . . Must not . . . Must . . . Must not. Then, about the time the long black line had everything in such good order that even the sheriff could not complain, the voting window would close for the day.

"I'm a segregationist," Baker commented, "but if I was a nigger I'd be doing exactly what they are doing." Following the Selma troubles, Wilson Baker was elected to succeed Clark as sheriff of Dallas County. He died after serving six years.

Two churches were utilized in the Selma demonstration—Brown's Chapel for adults and another three blocks away for the young people, primarily school-aged from as young as ten to about eighteen. This group—boisterous, eager, and wanting to help—had its own meetings, and youngsters even attended some fairly structured classes in school routine. But what they liked to do most was to have ideas to further "The Movement."

During long hours of nothing to do, young black demonstrators often contrived new gimmicks for their part in the Selma Movement: "Let's sing all night." "Let's don't eat tomorrow." "Let's see if we can get somewhere without getting arrested." "Let's write a song." The crowd never lacked for ideas.

With young activists throughout the civil rights campaign, thoughts were never idle. At times of a standoff such as that in Selma, it was fairly certain that something unexpected was about to happen. These people simply could not sit still for very long.

One day in early March, one of the youngsters—or perhaps it was a group—came up with a brand new idea: "Let's walk to Montgomery and see the governor." That suggestion was greeted with no enthusiasm at all, which made absolutely no difference to those who gave the plan its birth and inspiration. The leadership was against the venture; federal authorities, who were trying to keep the demonstration on a sane path, were totally opposed. Word even came from the White House to discourage the idea, for President Johnson even then was planning his own solution: an all-out drive for passage of a new voting rights law that would affect every hamlet in America.

Montgomery was fifty miles away through sparsely-settled rural country. Danger would be a constant companion for several hundred blacks with no place to stay overnight, and with no security. Furthermore, it would be a wearying experience that would sap the strength of the entire Selma Movement.

By the next day, however, the plan was being talked about all over the Selma camp. People said they were going, with or without Dr. King's permission. Finally, as often happened in dealing with his "children," King capitulated, and the Selma-to-Montgomery walk was authorized to begin. The date was set for Sunday, March 7. By then, scores of outsiders were attracted to the little Alabama town to participate in this symbolic adventure.

Although he had approved the march, King apparently thought that it would be only another symbolic gesture not requiring his presence. He left town, naming his first assistant, the Reverend Ralph David Abernathy, to represent the Southern Christian Leadership Conference in getting the walk started.

Members of the Selma Movement were in the front line as it formed that Sunday in the street outside Brown's Chapel. The mood was serious, for there had been advance warning of trouble. Quietly, the word was passed to march, and the line moved toward town, down Broad Street to the river bridge at the edge of town.

Highway 80 out of Selma is east on Broad Street across the Pettus Bridge, a concrete and steel structure that spans the Alabama River. On the Montgomery side of the bridge at least fifty state troopers waited, having been sent by Governor George Wallace to stop "an unlawful assembly." The state police were augmented by fifteen of Sheriff Jim Clark's deputies on horseback. As the marchers came to the Pettus Bridge, an amplified voice commanded them to stop. They obeyed.

"This is Major Cloud. This is an unlawful assembly. Your march is not conducive to safety. You are to disperse and go back to your church or to your homes."

Hosea Williams, a brash black activist in the lead of the marchers, tried to speak to Cloud. He was cut off: "There is no word to be had. You have two minutes to go back to your church." The marchers prayed; then they started walking slowly, east toward their goal. The next voice: "Troopers advance."

Horsemen plunged into the crowd, clubs and whips swinging. It required only a few moments to break the march into total confusion. The marchers straggled and limped back to Brown's Chapel, bruised, and choked by tear gas. The entire episode was the Sunday night fare on national television despite efforts of authorities to keep reporters at a distance. Laurens Pierce, a CBS cameraman, waded through the tear gas, dodged the horses, and filmed the whole incident. Winding up the assault, troopers advanced on Brown's Chapel itself, routing occupants with tear gas, nightsticks, and drawn guns, herding them toward their homes.

King was staggered by the news. He said he had no idea that the march would be halted with such ferocity. He declared that he would lead a new march out of Selma in just two days. On Tuesday, March 9, King kept his promise. But again he had been given advance information that the second march would be only a face-saving exercise. This was to be a negotiated symbol. March leaders, state troopers, and federal mediators agreed that King and a crowd of fifteen hundred could cross the bridge, walk a mile toward Montgomery, and at that point be turned back by state police. It happened that way without incident, and the blacks peacefully dispersed. LeRoy Collins of the Federal Community Relations Service met with both sides ahead of time to mediate the arrangement. President Johnson personally persuaded King not to go through with a major demonstration—that day.

It was at this stage that the governor of Alabama asked to meet with the president, and President Johnson agreed. They talked in Washington for three hours. After the meeting, Governor Wallace said he would permit the march to Montgomery if he were so ordered by a court.

In a federal hearing that followed, Alabama state police testified before District Judge Frank M. Johnson, Jr., in Montgomery that the march would be hazardous because of heavy traffic and wooded areas along the route.

The federal judge was then given minute details of the proposed march, including a plan for each day:

Day One, eleven miles, stop in private field, permission granted;
Day Two, eleven miles, stop in field, permission granted;
Day Three, seventeen miles, stop at a building and field, permission granted;
Day Four, eight miles to western edge of Montgomery;
Day Five, into town.

Every street out of Selma and into Montgomery was indicated, as well as all services to be provided for the marchers. The court approved the plan. The word was: Go! And thus ended phase one of the Selma adventure. On with the march!

Marchers participating in the Selma to Montgomery civil rights march walk past a white youth holding a Confederate flag on March 21, 1965. Photo: © Bettmann-Corbis

CHAPTER 13

1965–The Selma Story, Part 2

"For, lo, the winter is past; the rain is over and gone."

—Song of Solomon

On March 15, 1965, President Johnson called on Congress to adopt legislation that would "strike down restrictions to voting in all elections—federal, state, and local—which have been used to deny Negroes the right to vote."

The president said, "The time for waiting is gone," referring without mentioning Selma by name, to continuing thwarted voting efforts by blacks in the South, and to "the outraged conscience of a nation." This was a clear reference to what happened eight days before when Selma, Alabama, blacks, trying to make their walk to the state capital in Montgomery to put their voting requests before Governor George Wallace, were attacked by club-wielding officers.

Leaning on the Fifteenth Amendment to the Constitution that guaranteed the right to vote, Johnson asked for legislation that aroused sharp criticism in and out of Congress. It was like stirring a hornet's nest. Southerners in the Senate cried that the bill was unconstitutional and punitive. Liberals in both houses sought to use the new legislation to wipe out all vestiges of the poll tax in state and local elections, still required in twenty-seven states. (Only Alabama, Mississippi, Texas, and Virginia still used it in 1965 as a voter qualification).

On the 18th of March, the Senate sent the Johnson bill to the Judiciary Committee headed by Senator James O. Eastland, Mississippi Democrat and determined foe of any civil rights legislation. Recognizing Eastland's ability to bottle up bills he didn't want, the Senate instructed the committee to pass the measure out to the Senate floor by April 9, prompting Eastland to shout that "it is an unheard-of thing to permit only fifteen days to study so far-reaching a bill." Eastland must have remembered back to just a year before when he was also bypassed on civil rights legislation.

In Selma, meanwhile, planning went forward for the big march to Montgomery, now formally approved by a federal judge. Selma blacks were in a daze from the fast-moving developments. Governor Wallace advised federal authorities on March 20 that the state could not protect the marchers. Now, at last, with the feds willing for the march to happen, President Johnson promptly ordered the Alabama National Guard into the U.S. Army. The marchers had their protection.

The president said that if this group of black people wanted to walk along a highway in America, they had every right to do so, and the United States government would guarantee that right. The federalized National Guard would be used to see to it. Commanding the military phase of the operation was Brigadier General Henry V. Graham, assistant commander of the 31st National Guard Division. It was he who had earlier led a federalized National Guard onto the campus of the University of Alabama.

On Sunday, March 21, at 12:45 p.m., the march from Selma to Montgomery assembled for the third time. From a few hundred in the first attempt, and 1,500 in the second, the crowd had swelled to more than 3,000 including a number of white sympathizers. In the lead were Dr. Martin Luther King, Jr.; Ralph Abernathy, his assistant; Paul R. Screvane, president of the New York City Council; Constance Baker Motley, president of the Manhattan (N.Y.) Borough, an attorney who won many civil rights victories in court; and Dr. Ralph Bunche, United Nations undersecretary and holder of the 1950 Nobel Peace Prize for mediating a 1949 Palestinian conflict between Israel and Arab nations. Grandson of slaves, he was the first black to win the award.

King sent them adventuring with these words: "Those of us who are Negroes don't have much; we don't have much education, and some of us don't know how to make our nouns and verbs agree. But thank God, we have our bodies, our feet and our souls. Walk together, children. Don't you get weary, and it will lead us to the Promised Land, and Alabama will be a new Alabama, and America will be a new America."

As the huge delegation stepped off from Brown's Chapel, the mood was light and jovial in contrast to past fear. The Reverend Ralph David Abernathy told followers: "When we get to Montgomery, we are going up to Governor Wallace's door and say: 'George, it's all over, we've got the ballot.'"

Most of the local blacks, never before accustomed to such a spectacle, could not believe it was happening to them after all those weeks in the mud and rain. Heads high, steps jaunty, some in song, some in prayer, they marched in a human wave toward Pettus Bridge, so recently to them a symbol of brutality. This was not just an ordinary bridge to them; Pettus was like a crossover from one world into another—from the pleasant streets of Selma to what soon became a rural highway to the state capital.

I watched them cross the bridge in their thousands, unmolested this time. The state troopers were still there, but now they only assisted in handling traffic on Jefferson Davis Highway (U.S. 80). The federalized National Guard was there. And as far as the eye could see U.S. Army troops were there. President Johnson let no mistake be made about this call-up. He sent almost four thousand troops to Highway 80, including five hundred military police, one hundred FBI agents, and one hundred U.S. marshals. John Doar, head of the Justice Department Civil Rights Division, walked the roadside for the entire march. After its initial show of great strength, the military stayed in the background, but close by in case of need.

The fifty-mile rural route to Montgomery was thoroughly scouted ahead of time. Representatives of LeRoy Collins' Community Relations office persuaded reluctant landowners, white and black, to make farms available for overnight stops. Food canteens were organized by the military. Daytime march schedules were organized. The marchers moved along Highway 80 in perfect safety. There was scarcely any traffic.

When the delegation reached the first night's campsite, four big tents already had been pitched on a black farmer's land. Cook fires were burning, and the smell of hot food drifted down the highway.

As the shades of night were drawn over the scene in middle Alabama, the outlines of hundreds of campers—farmers, students, educators, supporters from North and South—could be made out against the brown hillside of the farm eleven miles east of Selma. The rattling of cooking gear, the subdued voices of campers, the bustling about of their leaders, and the occasional sight of someone in a military uniform, gave the impression of an army bivouacked for the night. And so it was.

For the journalists reporting this extraordinary event, communication was all-important, and difficult. Houses were far apart, and residents were uneasy or outright afraid to let reporters in to use, the phone, at any price.

The little road junction town of Lowndesboro is about two-thirds of the way from Selma to Montgomery. I left the march there, looking for a telephone, and found a pay station at a cluster of stores. As I dictated material to my news bureau in Atlanta, the connection became weaker and weaker, until I was shouting—far too much noise for this particular spot. Presently, I heard a gruff male voice through the phone: "I think I know where he is. Let's go get him." The town had been listening. If anyone turned up, I was not there to greet them.

Some of us ordered shortwave radio equipment and set up base stations in Montgomery miles away where staff members took the calls and relayed the information on to distant news bureaus. Wire service correspondents had the worst problems, for, as a book about the business was titled, there's a *Deadline Every Minute*. News outlets in Asia, Africa, and Europe were eating up this story, just as they were in the United States.

Although King did not walk all of the fifty miles to Montgomery, he was there for the first day. From time to time after that, he made appearances at the head of the line, walked for a few miles, and then departed for destinations that were unknown to most of the marchers.

After the first day, the march lost some of its bounce. Sore feet and muscles took some of the fun out of the trip. March leaders patrolled the route constantly, watching for dropouts, encouraging the discouraged who wanted to go home long before the goal was in sight. But spirits rose at the end of each day. These people loved those campsites.

A surprise was in store for the wearying crowd on the fourth night. The campsite was on property of the City of St. Jude. The forty-acre Roman Catholic complex was the scene of an unbelievable entertainment that would have commanded top prices in a music hall: Symphony Orchestra Conductor Leonard Bernstein, acclaimed Gospel Singer Mahalia Jackson, Tony Bennett, Billy Eckstein, Sammy Davis, Jr., Dick Gregory, Joan Baez, the song team of Peter, Paul and Mary, Lena Horne, and Harry Bellafonte gave their best in support of the marchers.

There's a line in the musical, *Pearlie*: "Black people have lots of fun, if there ain't nobody looking." A black preacher in Atlanta, Georgia, put it another way. Aroused by a powerful hymn in his church one Sunday, he stretched out his arms and shouted: "Lord, I'm so glad I'm black." The blacks had unreserved fun that night at St. Jude's.

On the fifth day, marchers rounded a sharp curve with Dr. King in the lead, and moved down Montgomery's Dexter Avenue, past the little Baptist church where the black leader got his start, along the route that Jefferson Davis rode to his inauguration as president of the Confederate States of America, to an area directly in front of the state capitol.

Six Roman Catholic nuns had come from St. Louis, Missouri, to lend their backing to the walk; educators, day laborers from East and West, college students, and school children, all were caught up in the euphoria of an unforgettable moment.

One of the marchers was Dr. Henry R. Winkler, at that time history professor at Rutgers University, later executive vice president of Rutgers, and still later president of the University of Cincinnati. He walked between historians Walter Johnson and John Hope Franklin, chairman of the Department of History at Howard University and author of *From Slavery to Freedom*. With them were such eminent academicians as C. Vann Woodward, Sterling Professor of History at Yale and author of *The Strange Career of Jim Crow*, and Kenneth M. Stampp, Oxford, Berkeley, and Maryland historian. In all there were forty-five historians. As Winkler recalled the experience to me, these highlights remained imbedded in his memory:

"They were not, as the late Richard Hofstadter put it neatly, if embarrassingly, bearded youths or excitable junior faculty members, but mature viewers of American history, 'professors with sagging midriffs.'

"Why, then, should such a company of people drop their work, plunge their hands into their own pockets, fly to Atlanta, bounce a hundred miles cross-country in an antiquated children's school bus, sleep for two or three hours, and then march with perhaps 20,000 other people over the last few miles of a journey whose earlier miles were the ones which required courage and sacrifice?

"They felt it important because they believed as responsible citizens in the goal of equal rights for blacks and whites. They knew as scholars how desperately harmful to our entire society is the degradation of a part of that society, harmful to the quality of our life here at home, harmful to the influence and effectiveness of our country throughout the world.

"They recognized that people of courage and wisdom—in the South as in the rest of the country—were beginning to sense that we have reached the end of an era—that the dream of equal citizenship rights for Americans, while it may yet be far off, may become a reality, if only people of good intentions will work toward it."

As I walked around the curve of Highway 80 going into downtown Montgomery, thoughts flashed back to those days and nights on the march: the army-guarded campsites, the calls for medical help to ease the pain of blistered feet, and the sheer improbability of the accomplishment of these people who had no power but their bodies and their commitment.

The marchers were met at the speakers' platform, erected in the middle of Dexter Avenue, by Ralph Bunche of the United Nations, Roy Wilkins of the NAACP, A. Phillip Randolph, president of the Union of Sleeping Car Porters, veteran Civil Rights Strategist Bayard Rustin, John Lewis of the Student Non-Violent Coordinating Committee, and thousands who had not made the entire march. The crowd had now swelled to almost thirty thousand, all because a while ago two hundred blacks were refused permission to walk Highway 80 from Selma to Montgomery.

The demonstration leaders tried twice that afternoon to see the governor, who was in the trooper-guarded state capitol one-half block away. Twice they failed to present Wallace with a petition. This was their statement:

"When the course of human events denies the citizens of this nation the right to vote, the right to an adequate education, an opportunity to earn sufficient income, and when Negro channels for real change are both slow and costly, the people must turn to rights provided by the first Amendment to the Constitution. We must appeal to the seat of government with the only peaceful and non-violent resources at our command: our physical presence and the moral power of our souls . . . We are here because for over 100 years our Constitutionally-guaranteed right to vote has been abridged . . . We call upon you, Governor Wallace, to declare your faith in the American creed, to declare your belief in the words of the Declaration of Independence that all men are created equal . . . We call upon you to establish democracy in Alabama."

Dr. Martin Luther King, Jr., spoke to the masses in the street:

"Our bodies are tired, and our feet are somewhat sore, but today as I stand before you and look back over that great march, I can say as Sister Pollard, a seventy-year-old Negro woman, said, who lived in this community during the bus boycott. One day she was asked while walking if she did not want a ride. When she answered 'No,' the person said, 'Well, aren't you tired?' And with her ungrammatical profundity, she said, 'My feets is tired, but my soul is rested.'

"They told us we wouldn't get here, and there were those who said we would get here over their dead bodies. But all the world today knows that we are here, and that we are standing before the sources of power in the state of Alabama, saying, 'We ain't going to let nobody turn us around.'"

The cheers that greeted this remark rolled up Dexter Avenue like a mighty tidal wave, and must have resounded through every corridor of the capitol.

"How long? Not long, because no lie can live forever," King proclaimed. "How long? Not long, because you still reap what you sow. How long? Not long, because the arm of the moral universe is long, but it bends to justice. How long? Not long because:

"Mine eyes have seen the glory of the coming of the Lord; He is trampling out the vintage where the grapes of wrath are stored; He hath loosed the fateful lightning of His terrible swift sword; His truth is marching on.

"He has sounded forth the trumpet that shall never sound retreat; He is sifting out the hearts of men before His judgment seat; O be swift, my soul, to answer Him! Be jubilant, my feet!"

Toward the end of the three-and-a-half hour rally, King told the crowd: "We are not about to turn around. We are on the move now. No wave of racism can stop us. Let us march on segregated schools until every vestige of segregation and inferior education becomes a thing of the past, and Negroes and whites study side by side in the socially-healing context of the classroom. Let us march on ballot boxes until race baiters disappear from the political arena . . . Our aim must never be to defeat or humiliate the white man, but to win his friendship and understanding . . . My people, my people. Listen, the battle is in our hands."

So it was in Montgomery, Alabama, at the conclusion of the famed Selma to Montgomery march. The event had gone off without a hitch. It had easily been one of the most dramatic events of the entire civil rights campaign. The crowds melted away in the late afternoon inspired and feeling good, despite their sore feet.

Viola Liuzzo Killed on the Road Home

One last time, just before dark, I checked the radio communications shack of the State Highway Patrol. All was quiet everywhere, the police reported. People were dispersing peacefully. Special flights were leaving the Montgomery airport—with delegations from distant corners of the nation who had come to Selma to lend their presence to the march. Buses waited to transport the Selma people home.

One of the volunteers did not make it home. Viola Gregg Liuzzo, 39, a Detroit, Michigan, housewife and mother of five, came to Alabama after telling her husband, "I must do something." She was assigned to transportation service for Selma demonstrators. She was shot to death from a roadside ambush one mile from Lowndesboro as she was returning to Montgomery after delivering a group of blacks to Selma following the march. A black youth in the car with her played dead and escaped to report the killing.

Until then it had seemed to be a peaceful ending to that arduous fifty-mile walk from Selma. One of our best staffers, Nick Chriss, volunteered to check out the story. When he failed to return within a reasonable time, another staffer was sent down the dark highway. He soon returned with word from officers guarding a short bridge on the road that an unidentified white reporter had been arrested and jailed. I knew it had to be Nick so I dropped everything and went for him.

The county seat of Lowndesboro, about midway between Selma and Montgomery, is awake at dawn but very dark at night. There was a phone number to call after hours to confirm that Nick was locked up. I would have to contact the county judge in the morning. No sense in driving back to Montgomery at 3 a.m. so I just hunkered down in the locked car and waited for dawn.

Promptly at 9 a.m. I was at the judge's desk in the back of a typical country store. He was not unfriendly, just all business, there at his roll top desk. He handed me a signed release form and said the fine would be fifty dollars. I didn't ask the judge what my prisoner had done, but he told me—speeding. I paid. Nick, who was still almost speechless when his jailer released him, confirmed the paper. "I was scared to death," he said.

Four white men, members of the Ku Klux Klan, were arrested and charged with Mrs. Liuzzo's murder. Their arrests were announced personally by President Johnson at a hastily-called televised news conference in Washington. The president, his voice shaking with emotion and anger, labeled the suspects—Eugene Thomas, 43; William O. Eaton, 41; Gary Thomas Rowe, Jr., 31; and Collie Leroy Wilkins, Jr., 21—members of "a society of bigots."

"My father fought the Ku Klux Klan many long years ago in Texas, and I have fought them all my life because I believe them to threaten the peace of every community where they exist," the president said.

Thomas, Eaton, and Wilkins were tried, but their cases twice ended in mistrials in state court and they went free. In December of 1965, however, an all-white federal jury convicted Thomas, Eaton, and Wilkins of conspiracy to violate Mrs. Liuzzo's civil rights. Federal Judge Frank M. Johnson sentenced them to the maximum ten-year sentence allowed by the charge.

Again President Johnson spoke out on the case: "The whole nation can take heart from the fact that there are those in the South who believe in justice in racial matters and who are determined not to stand for acts of violence and terror."

In 1978, an Alabama grand jury returned a murder indictment against Rowe, an FBI informer who was riding in the car and provided the information on which the three other men were arrested. A federal judge ruled that Rowe could not be prosecuted because he had been promised federal immunity.

Four days after the conclusion of the big march, and three days after arrest of suspects in the slaying of Mrs. Liuzzo, St. Paul's Episcopal Church in Selma seated three black worshipers from Selma and one from Boston, Massachusetts.

While the drama and the tragedy of Selma were being played out and relayed via national television, in Washington the House and Senate debated the administration's voting rights bill. The measure finally came down to agreement on a compromise bill on July 29. The deadlock of the long debate was broken when civil rights groups urged the House to drop a proposal calling for an outright ban on poll taxes in state and local elections—a provision that President Johnson had strongly desired.

The poll tax had already been eliminated from federal elections. President Kennedy supported a constitutional amendment in 1962 to do that, and the amendment passed both houses of Congress. After ratification by three-fourths of the states, it became the Twenty-fourth Amendment to the U.S. Constitution in 1964. The civil rights people feared, however, that the rigidity of extending the poll tax ban to local elections could defeat the entire act.

In its final form the poll tax provision that was approved in the new act simply established that the levy constituted an abridgement of the right to vote, and it directed the attorney general to initiate court action against enforcement of the tax. The House also agreed to a Senate version stipulating that no one could be denied the right to vote because of inability to read or write in English, provided he or she could demonstrate completion of the sixth grade.

The heart of the 1965 act was the provision that it would apply to all elections, down to the local level. When it came to a final vote, 111 Republicans and 217 Democrats in the House—thirty-seven of those Democrats from the South—approved the measure. In the Senate, thirty Republicans and forty-nine Democrats—six from the South—voted in favor. Praising the action by Congress, President Johnson said it brought "within our immediate vision the day when every American can enter a polling booth without fear or hindrance."

The president signed the bill into law on August 6, 1965, saying that the act would "strike away the last major shackle of the Negro's ancient bonds."

During the next eighteen years, Selma "made tremendous progress," as it was put to me by a Selma official whose experience spanned the era of violence and change. "You would have to see how it is today as opposed to the sixties," he said. "While we are not perfect, we feel we have had more racial progress than any city I know of."

According to my information, out of eleven city councilmen in 1983 in Selma, five were black, and blacks served on almost all municipal boards. They were about equally divided with white members on school and library boards. There was a black assistant chief of police, and blacks served as department heads in city government for sanitation, federal programs, code enforcement, personnel, and others.

From a voter registration in 1965 of 9,800 white and 275 black, the official record in 1983 was 16,508 black and 18,220 white voter registrants. All public facilities, schools, motels, hotels, restaurants, recreation facilities, and the Chamber of Commerce membership roll had been opened to all races—without exception.

A burning trash can rolls over the curb as police officers and demonstrators clash in Harlem on June 17, 1963. Some twenty-five youths were arrested during the disturbance. Photo: © Bettmann-Corbis

CHAPTER 14

1964–The South Is Not Alone

"God damn white man"
Is nothing sacred?   —Signs on street in New York City

"I have heard something said about allegiance to the South. I know
no South, no North, no East, no West, to which I owe any allegiance.
The Union, sir, is my country."

—Henry Clay

Traveling the South in early 1953 to research the background of the civil rights story that was in the making, I stopped at a small cabin on the vast flat delta of the Mississippi River. Here, blacks since the days of slavery had plowed, planted, and picked cotton for landlords and masters they rarely if ever saw. An elderly black man was sitting on the porch in the shade.

All day, I had driven through this storied plantation country and had been struck by a perplexing factor: there were very few children. So I asked the man on the porch: "Where are all the children?"

"They gone north," he responded readily. "They getting educated. But soon as they can, they be back; they be coming home."

Thousands of Southern blacks left the land when racial discrimination was almost absolute. When barriers of segregation began to topple in the South, many who had gone North or West to escape restrictions and to find advantages for their children, did indeed come home.

Economic advantages and education had been the attractions for them; what so many discovered in the big cities of the North and West was a brand of prejudice as offensive as that they had left in the deep South. They found evidence of an old saying that in the North the Negro was loved as a race and hated and feared as an individual, while in the South he was loved as an individual and despised and feared as a race.

Southern blacks were accustomed to "de facto" segregation, which means existing as the controlling power—repulsive to them but easy to understand. Now they were being introduced to what the lawyers call "de jure" discrimination in which legal rights were not the issue; practices were.

In the summer of 1964, with the new national Civil Rights Act in place, I went to New York on assignment by UPI to determine, if possible, and report on the causes of recent race-connected riots in the city. Reasons were not difficult to find. In New York—like many other large cities outside the South—where schools and public facilities had been desegregated all along, there were problems that the new laws did not touch.

New York was long a festering place of racial discord, although the city had some of the most liberal and humane statutes anywhere, long before there was a new Civil Rights law from the Congress. Conditions grew steadily worse as Southern blacks, escaping from poverty, unequal opportunities, or white wrath, poured into the big city looking for jobs, food, and shelter. Supposed competition for the necessities sometimes provoked the same vicious outbursts that took place in the South over social issues.

Standing atop a new apartment building at 98th Street and Park Avenue in upper Manhattan, I had a clear view of the famous boulevard that connects two worlds. At 98th Street, the New York Central train roared out of its underground line to take the elevated route across the Harlem River. The view of Park Avenue toward downtown Manhattan was one of penthouses and elegance; the view uptown was wash hanging on lines strung between fire escapes, and Harlem's asphalt jungle.

There were no physical barriers separating the two worlds of Park Avenue on its zigzag course around the ghetto of Harlem. But to the 235,000 blacks who lived there then—almost the total black population of Richmond, Virginia, at the time—the economic and social barricade was as clear as any Dixie sign that specified "white only." The fight in Harlem was not against segregated schools and eating places, but against what Harlemites called "The System," "The Man," and "Whitey."

Charles Connors, a black teacher at a junior high school in New York's Harlem, was one of almost three hundred individuals, white and black, selected in random interviews across the nation during a UPI study of the racial situation in 1963. In many ways Connors summed up what I heard from many blacks at the scene of racial demonstrations all over the eastern United States.

"What do I want?" he asked. "Not to be singled out as something special. That's what most Negroes want—to be treated like anyone else." He did not like the word integration. "I want people to be treated as people, to be judged on ability, not on whether their hair is long, short or kinky, or whether their eyes are blue or brown."

Thinking of Connors, I recalled the reaction in Columbia, South Carolina, when blacks won an important concession—to be addressed as Mister or Mrs., and the right to try on hats in stores. All they wanted was a little dignity—not to be called "You" or something else, but to be addressed as "Mister" or "Mrs." and not to be told by a clerk, "If you touch that hat, it's yours."

There was often the cry of police brutality when officers came into the ghetto to break up trouble or to make an arrest. Yet, the term "brutality" seemed to be an apt description of "The System" as some blacks in the New York ghetto viewed it. Theirs was a struggle to belong; they felt that progress, despite all the laws and the attention being given to the black plight, was agonizingly slow. The blacks in Harlem were frustrated, and that frustration often gave way to despair, despair to hatred, and hatred to violence against the established order.

"You ask me why I want to move," said a black mother of three children living in a row of old tenements on 111th Street just off Fifth Avenue. "It stinks in there; that's why. And there is no escape. I just want to escape."

"Whitey needs to get it in his mind that this is not against the white man," said a Negro standing in front of a splintered plate glass window that had been smashed by rioters the week before. "This is a rebuke to the power structure. This crowd that yells 'kill the white man' is just a fringe group aspiring to get into the act. You can count them on one hand."

The days I walked the Harlem streets in 1964, blacks in the South were rejoicing over their new right to vote and ability to have a restaurant meal in integrated security; the signs of resentment still sent their messages in Harlem. "Go See Blood Feast" was scrawled in large crude letters on a flower urn on Lenox Avenue in the middle of Central Harlem.

The African Nationalist Freedom Council in America, quartered amidst many denominational sects with sidewalk churches, displayed a picture of a black Jesus with black disciples and a sign that read: "Go 'way Jordan, Let God's Chillun By. We Must Pass Over to the Promised Land or Die."

A black woman passed by the council headquarters and observed a big sign advertising a book entitled "The God Damn White Man." She muttered sadly to a friend, "Now, that just ain't right."

Militant blacks in New York, taking a cue perhaps from Southern blacks who sought to integrate churches on religious grounds, invaded famous Riverside Church one Sunday during morning services. Pushing past ushers, three blacks walked to the chancel in the presence of 1,500 startled worshippers, and presented a staggering list of demands: $500 million in reparations from churches and synagogues to be used for a Southern Lend Bank, publishing industries, television networks, community organizations, and communications training centers, black labor strike fund, a black university skills center, and assistance to a national welfare rights organization for blacks.

James Forman, who led the delegation into Riverside, told the congregation: "The Christian religion has instilled a concept in the older generation that we will have eternal life, and these kinds of ideas help perpetuate slavery. The richest man in the world, King James, wrote the Bible, and he probably wrote in that phrase about it being easier for a camel to go through the eye of a needle than for a rich man to get to Heaven. This is a perfect rationale to keep people poor."

Having said his piece, he and the delegation of blacks departed, leaving the worshippers thoroughly shocked. The New York mayor, John Lindsay, suggested that churches ring their chimes for police protection when threatened with disruptive activity. A *New York Times* editorial was headed: "Is Nothing Sacred?"

One hot summer day, I visited a racially tense neighborhood in New York and saw children idling around in the street. Two blocks away, I could see a magnificent swimming pool, almost empty. I asked an adult with me, "Why don't these kids go to the swimming pool?" The answer: "They could go there free, but they won't do it. That's somebody else's block; they are afraid to cross the line." Remember, this was 1964.

A companion to the turf conflict was vandalism: water fountains and restroom plumbing ripped from the walls, fires in classrooms, obscenities scrawled on buildings. Often, these acts of apparent malicious destruction, when they could be investigated, turned out to be acts of frustration, self-anger, or a deep sense of failure. I have known of students at the university level leaving an exam room to pound huge holes in a corridor wall. Frustration over failure.

Roy Wilkins of the National Association for the Advancement of Colored People recalled to me rather sadly that as a young man he worked very hard to get out of a ghetto where walls were covered with profane and obscene messages. "I finally made it into a Riverside Drive apartment, only to find the same kind of words in the elevators," he said.

Whatever it might be called, incidents like these in large cities outside the South usually were demonstrations against what the black participants termed "the power structure." While they had various grievances against the system, it usually boiled down to the charges that blacks got the first crack of a policeman's nightstick and the last of the jobs, housing, education, and public acceptance.

An argument between blacks and police officers often led to flashes of violence. Police were caught in the middle, facing accusations of brutality when they tried to break up riots from horseback with nightsticks. On a July night in St. Louis, for example, two officers answered an ambulance call for a black woman who said she was attacked trying to stop a fight between two of her teenage sons. The boys turned screaming on the police, attracting a large crowd. Before it was over, twelve officers were hurt. The National Guard was required to put down a riot in Rochester, New York, touched off by a police attempt to arrest an intoxicated black man at a street dance.

In Cleveland, Ohio, there is a predominantly black residential district called "Hough." One of the worst riots of the 1960s erupted in the district, primarily over housing. The area had been promised and had expected, a large government rebuilding program that would have provided better shelter. Instead, the money was used to start a downtown Cleveland project.

Adding to the climate of despair in Hough was what was viewed as an insensitive attitude on the part of city government. A black officer in a neighborhood improvement association showed me an example: a local school that had the community's only playing field. It had been surrounded by a high fence, and the school had orders to padlock the gates each day when school was out.

Most downtown Clevelanders knew little of actual conditions in Hough; some had never seen the place. With publicity continuing regarding the unrest in the area, however, there were those who determined to find out firsthand what was going on. The president of a large bank told his secretary one noon: "I'm going to Hough. I don't know what's happening there, but I'm going to find out." He did find out and went before the next meeting of the Cleveland Chamber of Commerce and told of the miserable conditions he found. His courage opened the way for quick downtown support for the area.

On August 11, 1965, the community of Watts in Los Angeles, California, was subjected to the worst ravaging by riots in the nation up to that time. Predominantly a black section of the huge city, in those days Watts was an island of despair in a bright and sparkling metropolis. Watts had no hospital within eight miles, and residents going outside the area to jobs had to transfer on buses three and four times. One out of four residents was on relief. "Federal relief has become a way of life," a Watts mother told me. "Everybody hates it, but we are trapped."

Many Watts blacks came out of the South during the years of World War II and held higher-paying jobs in the war plants than they had ever had back home. The climate was pleasant, racial discrimination was not a great problem—at least on the surface—and they thought this was the promised land. They wrote back home, and others followed. As the nation settled back to old ways after the war, blacks in Watts were in the same dilemma as thousands of others in cities of the North and West. In the competition for postwar jobs, they tended to be at the bottom of the heap; their living space was a huge gradually deteriorating ghetto.

Efforts by police to arrest a black man in the area was blamed for starting the Watts riot, but Watts black leaders charged that the fuse which lit the torch of violence was long-term exploitation. Many small- to medium-sized businesses lined the streets of Watts—grocery stores, shoe stores, clothing outlets, appliances, radio and television dealers, and repair shops. Many, if not most, were operated by absentee owners. As the facts regarding Watts' racial explosion began to emerge, most of the evidence pointed to exorbitant interest rates, excessive charges for time payments, and the vague (and always denied) charge of "police brutality."

Whether or not it was the realization in Watts of what was happening in the South and how demonstrations there had been partly responsible for a new Civil Rights Act in Congress, the fact was that Watts was a festering sore of bitterness and defeat. The agony of Watts burst into action on the night of August 11 when the first rocks and firebombs went through store windows. Before the orgy was brought under control five days later, the toll was 35 dead, 883 injured, fire damage of $175 million, and property damage of $46 million.

Stores were methodically picked for destruction, almost always by the criterion of real or imagined exploitation. Within a block of fire-ravaged ruins, a building would be left standing and unharmed by either fire or vandals. "The folks in there were good to us," a Watts black said to me of these places during a tour of the devastation. I saw the hot embers of some places that had been torched, not once or twice but three and four times until the very ashes were reburned. The bitterness against some of the merchants was that intense.

"Burn, baby, burn" was the by-word of the Watts rioters. They not only burned but they violently resisted efforts by police and firemen to curb their anger. Firemen racing from blaze to blaze were common targets of snipers. Wholesale looting was Watts' answer to unfulfilled expectations. Trucks, carts, and human backs were openly used to haul away whatever was available once the windows were smashed, and before the fire got to its work.

The Watts blacks wanted to handle their statement to the nation in their own way; they sought no help from the organized civil rights groups. Just after the fires burned out, Dr. Martin Luther King, Jr., went to Watts to offer his support toward the realization of civil rights goals. In his meeting with Watts blacks, I observed that his reception was cool.

Looking back through notes of other big-city assignments during racial troubles, I came upon an interview with Tredfik Bey, a black Chicago insurance agent who was president of the Concerned Parents of Chicago's West Side. When that city's worst riot in half a century erupted, Bey worked for one hundred hours without rest to cool down the trouble.

"Some of these people believe there is no hope," he said. "I am trying to show them there is hope. We must rebuild this community from the ground up, and we—the people who live here—must get out there and do it. I think we are more ready to do the job than ever before. It is not frustration that causes people to blow up. It's desperation. Because they have nothing to live for anyway, when something bad happens they go completely to pieces and lose all control of themselves. We've got to find a way to stop that."

Bey's statement, it seems to me, best explains the terrible and deepest motive for destroying one's own environment. As observer-reporter of more than one such scene, I would agree it was hopelessness and desperation that lit the torch.

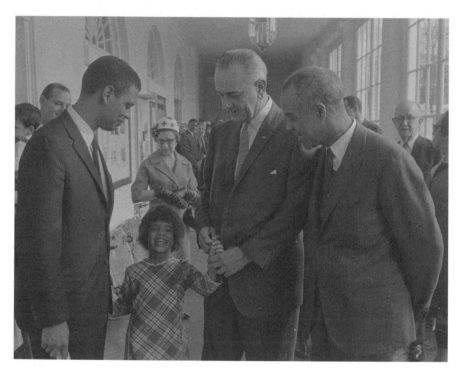

Roy Wilkins (right), executive director of the National Association for the Advancement of Colored People, watches as his nephew, Roger Wilkins, a thirty-three-year-old New York lawyer (left), introduces his six-year-old daughter, Amy, to President Johnson. They talked with Johnson after Roger Wilkins was sworn in as director of the Community Relations Service at a White House ceremony on February 4, 1966. Photo: © Bettmann-Corbis

CHAPTER 15

1966–Black Leader Roy Wilkins Speaks Out

"There is no turning back."   —Roy Wilkins

"If you would hit the mark, you must aim a little above it."

—Henry Wadsworth Longfellow

November 10, 1966. Roy Wilkins, executive vice president of the National Association for the Advancement of Colored People (NAACP), gazed thoughtfully toward a balloon of storm clouds on the horizon and said, "Yes, the promised land is still a long way off." Then, hesitating only a moment, he added intently, "But there's much more of it in view now; we can see where we are going."

Wilkins in 1966 was in charge of keeping in operation the far-flung, and sometimes perilous, activities of the NAACP. His job also involved a constant re-evaluation of progress and problems. The NAACP was a movement he had joined as a young man in Kansas City, Kansas, leaving behind a promising newspaper career. It became his life's work.

On that day in November, I met Wilkins in Birmingham, Alabama, and flew with him to his business appointment in Jackson, Mississippi. The flight provided an insight into the thinking of the NAACP leader that might profitably be shared with readers of later decades. This particular profile of a black leader from the turbulent 1960s was chosen because of Wilkins' long association with and commitment to the organization that was the predecessor of most other civil rights groups.

Wilkins was fond of telling militant newcomers to the anti-segregation effort that the NAACP pioneered what they later adopted. He would tell them that the NAACP Youth Council held the first sit-ins in Oklahoma City, Oklahoma, two years before four college students "originated" the idea in Greensboro, North Carolina. Continuing his NAACP history lesson, he would remind youngsters that he went to work for the organization in 1932, but that the first jail-ins were in 1918 and the first freedom rides in 1915. "So this is nothing new; it's just been refined," he said.

It was the NAACP, founded by a small group in a tiny New York apartment in 1909, which led the battle against lynching and Ku Klux Klan activities when no others, black or white, inveighed against them. It was the NAACP that fought racial prejudice from the film studios of Hollywood to the back roads of the South long before events of the 1960s. The 1954 public school desegregation decision of the U.S. Supreme Court, after twelve years of shaky implementation, was now being accepted and followed. The 1964 Civil Rights Act and the 1965 Voting Rights Act, guaranteeing blacks the same public and legal rights as whites, were in place and working. The NAACP could take much of the credit for these legal victories.

Soon after our plane took off from Birmingham into the darkening skies, I asked Wilkins: "Where do Negroes stand now? Are you past Sinai?" The analogy was not a new one, nor lost on Wilkins. The transition and shift in the lot of U.S. blacks had often been likened to the Exodus of the Israelites from Egypt. A spiritual popular in black churches and sung repeatedly during racial meetings in the South, says: "Go down Moses, way down to Egypt land; tell old Pharoah to let my people go."

Religion more than politics was the power plant of the civil rights thrust of the mid-twentieth century, and indeed long before. Almost all of its leaders and the bulk of its followers came through the churches. The songs, the soaring oratory, the generally unified action all had roots in the deep faith of black church congregations. The famous battle hymn of the racial campaign, "We Shall Overcome," was a spiritual long before it was introduced into the civil rights drive.

"Yes, we're beyond Mount Sinai," Wilkins said with a smile. "We've got the Ten Commandments, and we're on the way. That's one thing you can say about today in contrast to other years. There's no turning back now. There are still battles to be fought, but it's a different kind of fight because we can see the Promised Land."

Wilkins survived the rough and tumble of the civil rights thrust of the 1960s to become one of the foremost elder statesmen of the black race, a man whose voice was respected in the White House, as well as in rural Mississippi, and in the narrow streets of Harlem in New York. Not everyone went along with him and the NAACP, of course. Some said he was too calm, too easy-going, too urbane, too slow. Some wanted action of the kind that filled the jails and sent crowds into the streets.

"I'm not against demonstrations if they serve a purpose." Wilkins said. "But we have to think of the overall results. Some of these folks pull off a big demonstration and fill the jail, then the NAACP has to bail them out." I often heard Wilkins condemned for statements like that.

The NAACP had always done much of the drudgery work of the civil rights movement—the work that produced few headlines. It raised the money to fight cases of discrimination through the courts for periods of up to ten years. And the organization worked tirelessly to establish a pattern in the country for educational programs in Negro voter registration, upgrading of jobs, and justice in the courts.

In earlier days, the NAACP was a bad name in much of the South. It was banned in one state, and in several others unsuccessful efforts were made to force the public release of membership lists. When more militant organizations came into being, however, the NAACP became regarded as almost moderate and won widespread respect.

Much of this changing attitude was due to Wilkins, who skillfully guided the organization through hectic years of transition. He withstood many pressures, both within and without the NAACP, to deliver its full strength into the street demonstrations. Despite this, Roy Wilkins was not a softie who let his adversary off the hook, as was sometimes charged. He had the courage to hang on like a terrier. It was that quality in him which helped to bring about victories like the Supreme Court school decision of 1954. The young NAACP-sponsored lawyers who led that fight did not get their training in the streets, but in the midnight glow of the study lamp.

Roy Wilkins' grandparents were slaves. His mother and father moved from Mississippi to St. Louis, Missouri, shortly after their marriage. Their children were sent to St. Paul, Minnesota, to live with relatives after Roy's mother died when he was three. It was a peaceful childhood for Roy.

After graduation from the University of Minnesota as a sociology major, he went to work for the *Kansas City Call*, a large Negro weekly newspaper, and soon became its managing editor. In Kansas City, Kansas, as a black he encountered difficulties that he had not known in his unrestricted life in St. Paul. His personal campaign against a Kansan campaigning for the U.S. Senate in 1930 brought Wilkins to the attention of the NAACP board of directors, which led to his appointment to the agency's staff. He succeeded the late Walter White as executive vice president in 1955, the year after the Supreme Court decision outlawing racial segregation in the public schools.

"Most of the civil rights activity up to then was in faith," Wilkins told me during our plane ride. "The school decision was one of the great landmarks. It was an unequivocal affirmation for the first time of the constitutional rights of Negroes as citizens. The decision simply said there could not be two standards. Up to then, the status of the Negro had been at the whim of every interpreter, North and South. After 1954, it was 'go for the downs.'

"This decision opened up a whole new world. So, I say we are far ahead today, and not only just Negroes. We have white allies today, North and South, by the thousands, who were not with us a few years ago. One thing that helped us was the solid support for the first time from the three great religious branches—Protestant, Roman Catholic, and Hebrew. The Catholic action has been most important."

Wilkins saw far beyond the desegregation of schools and the opening of public facilities to blacks. He looked at the world and saw that it was mostly non-white. He looked at the fast-developing communications sciences. "Nothing that happens in one country happens in a vacuum any more," he observed.

Wilkins' remarks returned with prophetic emphasis years after that long-ago flight. Two great nations—China and Japan—became world economic powers; the map of Africa completely changed with non-white revolutions. South Africa, twenty years after the Martin Luther King era, exploded in a black demand for total social integration and human rights that made the earlier American campaign pale by comparison. The deaths in that sad situation were in the uncounted hundreds.

I asked Roy Wilkins how he viewed the Black Power trend, with its brash and often violent tactics, that was beginning to infiltrate the civil rights effort. "I don't think Black Power bothers Asia and Africa," he said thoughtfully. "I suspect they don't view such a slogan with great alarm. But it has hurt very much in the United States. Black Power is a completely false issue. It was an unfortunate word usage at best. At worst, it was deliberately concocted as a rallying slogan by a group that wanted to startle and shock.

"Its exponents, after realizing the terrible reaction to it, began trying to explain what Black Power meant. They said it's political power, or economic power, or it was race pride. Well, all these things have been with us since the beginning of time. Race pride has been taught from the cradle. So, Black Power must have meant something else: an antagonistic means of achieving militant competition. This is a suicidal position, really. The Negro has lost the ball in the high grass if he tries to go it without the cooperation of the 90 percent majority in this country.

"Black Power is also totally out of step with the vast majority of Negro Americans. Most Negroes want into the American economy, not out of it. And I'll say this, we think it is happening too slowly, but the economy in America is beginning to say to Negroes: 'Come on in.'"

Wilkins was thinking ahead of his time but he had been like that as long as I had known him. He was one who always saw the light and seldom cursed the darkness. His voice at the most dismal times of the civil rights struggle—long before Dr. Martin Luther King, Jr., came into the picture—gave blacks inspiration to keep moving ahead. His was the audience of middle-class blacks trying to establish themselves in the mainstream, rather than the street people of later years. But he spoke to them, too, often in jail cells and county court-houses. Wilkins could feel forward movement in human rights just as a farmer can feel the swelling buds of a fruit tree in winter and know the sap is flowing.

As we talked, I pondered those words, "Come on in," and thought of the Southland. "Come on in" was not then yet the welcome sign in all of the South, but of course the South was not one place—never had been. It was easy to select places where the welcome mat was not yet out for blacks; but there were others. My hometown of Atlanta, Georgia, "the city too busy to hate," as the mayor put it, had come to terms with race, and blacks were moving up the economic scale, finding better housing, getting elected to public office.

I thought of the recently passed 1964 Civil Rights Act and the Voting Rights Act, and how they said beneath the legal jargon: "Come on in"—and how the 1964 act required businesses with federal contracts to state publicly, "We are an equal opportunity employer." It was new stuff for the South that was being mixed, and tested, and polished and was already beginning to be effective. In all his years plugging away at securing basic human rights for blacks, Wilkins never lost sight of the need for Negroes themselves to perform at their best, to stay in school and learn to compete on an equal footing rather than being given advantages with honeyed words and little substance. Wilkins' dream of blacks achieving competence and skills in the job market began to be realized in the South in the years after removal of traditional seg-regation barriers. But as we talked in 1966, the dream still had far to go. The mark had not then been reached.

"We don't have the number of trained and educated people needed, but this number is increasing steadily," he said with enthusiasm giving emphasis to his hope. "It will take time and hard work, but today, the Negro high school freshman knows—or should know—what is available to him, and he can dig in and prepare himself with some confidence."

Re-reading Wilkins' remarks later, I went to my file and pulled a folder labeled "Dr. Mordecai Johnson." Here was an interview with the president emeritus of Howard University in Washington, D.C. With the civil rights struggle reaching the boiling point in the South, I went to the Howard campus for a talk with Dr. Johnson. Born in the little town of Paris, Tennessee, at the end of his sixth grade there was no further schooling for black children. He traveled 132 miles to Nashville and entered the seventh grade. "It was the first time I had come in contact with white people who expected high moral responsibility from Negroes," he said. "The teachers addressed themselves not to what I was but to what I could become."

As we walked along a university path, Dr. Johnson reflected on the importance of respect between the races, and he felt on that day in the early 1960s that it was beginning to happen in the South.

"We need to make the South Exhibit A to show the world what America's attitude is toward the Negro," he said. "When a person comes to us from another land and says 'How do you treat the Negroes?' we can take them to Atlanta or Little Rock or Jackson, Mississippi, and be honored to show them. Instead of apologizing for Georgia and Mississippi, we will want to show Atlanta as a place where under great difficulty and on slave soil we are making men of the children of disadvantage. One of these days we will say to Africa, 'You go to Little Rock and see how we treat Negroes.'"

The conversation with Dr. Johnson ended with an appeal to his Southern home from this great black educator: "I am asking the South to love these people, however crude they may be, and say 'I am going to take the responsibility for making them great. They are going to learn—here and from me.'"

Roy Wilkins was also fighting the same battle for the same kind of understanding; everywhere he went he told stories of black successes to young blacks who had not yet experienced success.

He would recall President Johnson's appointment of Andrew Brimmer, a black man, to the Federal Reserve Bank Board. "Here was a Negro, born down on the Mississippi-Louisiana border. They found him on the faculty at the Wharton School of Finance of the University of Pennsylvania. He was a whiz at figures. They put him in the Department of Commerce working on the balance of payments world trade problem. In a short time, he helped cut the imbalance by a billion dollars. So, they moved him up to the Federal Reserve Board, not because he was a black man but because he was a capable man."

I asked Wilkins to draw on his long experience and provide a composite attitude held by blacks after their recent hard-won victories. He was quite thoughtful for some minutes before giving this evaluation: "Negroes are wishful and hopeful at the same time. But they are still aware of too many setbacks and denials to be wholly optimistic about the future yet. Generally, however, we feel we are getting ahead and that we will do better in the future. I would say the Negro is more determined than ever today. He feels he must have what is coming to him, but he doesn't want—and shouldn't have—more than is due him as a human being." The NAACP chief paused, looked out the plane window and then turned to me with more than his usual spirit. "As for respect," he said, "the Negro is not requesting it any longer; he is demanding it. He is not quite clear how he will get it, but he knows one thing. He doesn't want it to be withheld for another fifty years. He doesn't want people telling him any more to 'go slow.' This is an across-the-board attitude, and I want to emphasize that."

Our plane dropped down out of the clouds, and the skyline of downtown Jackson, the state capital, came into view. Wilkins was silent for awhile, and I felt he was thinking of past days in Mississippi: the desperately deprived condition of blacks, their inability to vote, the murder of Medgar Evers, his friend who was the NAACP field secretary in Mississippi, the moving funeral for Evers and what Wilkins called the "senseless" rioting by young blacks that followed.

So, too, was I lost in thought momentarily. Somewhere down there in Mississippi was a small plot of land beside a dirt road. It once held a little black church. I remembered the morning before dawn that I was directed to the spot in time to feel the still-hot ashes. I remembered the minister standing there in shock, not able to believe that someone had torched the church. As the plane circled the city, Wilkins took a deep breath as though erasing unpleasant thoughts from his mind.

"Now, about the white people," he continued. "They are still woefully misinformed about the Negro. This is partly due to the whole structure of education and its downgrading of the Negro in history. It's also partly due to the mass news media which presents only the story of conflict and division. The Negro who goes berserk and shoots up a white man is news, but the ten thousand who go about their normal jobs are never noticed."

Here it was again: The news media, and this time from one of its friends, a former member of the "club." But it was true. The news of these events had been blown out of focus at times by eager, mostly honest news people, competing to be first with the story, pressured by some editor far from the scene.

I was not blameless in looking for the spectacular. The fact that nothing happened today was never the ingredient for a headline or a newscast. The news media are never perfect, yet I shudder to think of the alternative to a free press.

The plane touched the runway and began to taxi slowly to the terminal, but there was more that Wilkins wanted to say. "You know what I feel?" and now the tone of his voice was suddenly buoyant and joyful. "I feel that much of the problems have been in the South in the past, but there is significant understanding in the South today. It is time for the South to enter into a partnership with the Negro, and I want to urge that course of action. I think it is one of the great next steps in this movement."

Wilkins then came to a point that had often gotten him into trouble with some blacks: "We must turn the energies of Negroes into the fight against delinquency and crime, and for family stability and morality in its broadest sense. We must stop blaming white people and discrimination exclusively for all the ills. We must be willing to assume that some of the responsibility rests within the Negro group itself. We must seek to improve group behavior standards. We must get rid of the tendency to cover up for sins committed by Negro people. We need to deal with misconduct regardless of where it arises.

"It doesn't matter the color of your skin or whether you live in India or Indianola, Mississippi, there are certain rules men must live by. The civilized world must depend on these rules or else it can't survive. Truth, honesty, integrity, the ability to stand for what is right, and to condemn the wrong—these are the measures of a people."

The seat belt sign had gone off, and we joined other passengers in walking to the Jackson airport terminal. Before we said good-bye, Roy Wilkins made a final point: "Remember, the Negro can't be held to observance of these rules while he is being ruthlessly handled, and while his rights and dignity are being trampled. When you are kicking a man in the face, it's futile to tell him he ought to be a good citizen. But the Negro is emerging from conditions like that. It is time now that he shows some maturity, and that he realizes he is not going to be judged as a downtrodden black man.

"Some of the thoughtless acts of recent times have caused much of the so-called white backlash. When a white homeowner is watching television and sees on the screen Negroes rampaging in the streets, making faces at the camera and engaging in anti-social behavior, the white man says 'I don't want these people living in my neighborhood, and I'll do everything I can to keep them out.'"

Here Wilkins was expressing the attitude of a majority of white America. The black leader did know how people felt. A gesture by exuberant blacks, the wrong use of grammar, expression of a characteristic that was different from the accepted norm—all of these were translated by whites into what those sorts of actions would do to all of society. Never mind that whites had habits as unacceptable to blacks as the other way round. Without defending the wrong, Wilkins defended vigorously the right.

"The fact is that for every one of these people who misbehave, there are thousands of law-abiding Negroes going about the business of paying their bills, educating their children, going to church, and making good citizens. It is sad that the few have made it very hard for the many to truly overcome," said my fellow passenger on that flight to Jackson, Mississippi.

Dr. Martin Luther King, Jr., embraces nine-year-old Patricia Kinsey as he is greeted by school children and others at Mount Calvary Baptist Church in Newark, N.J., on March 27, 1968. King toured Newark seeking support for his upcoming Poor People's Campaign in Washington, D.C. Eight days later, King was dead. Photo: © Bettmann-Corbis

CHAPTER **16**

1968–King Is Dead, But His Dream Lives On

"This is not the end. It is not even the beginning of the end. But it is, perhaps, the end of the beginning."

—Winston Churchill

The roster of the Ebenezer Baptist Church in Atlanta listed Dr. Martin Luther King, Jr., as associate pastor. For some months during the decade of the civil rights revolution in the South, the church bulletin board facing busy Auburn Avenue contained these words: "A discontented man finds no easy chair."

Young Dr. King, whose father was the longtime pastor at Ebenezer, began his ministry at the Dexter Avenue Baptist Church in Montgomery, Alabama, but his work as a clergyman was soon overshadowed by his civil rights career. His discontent with racial barriers of any kind never stopped after the successful desegregation of Montgomery buses. With this commitment, he believed, and said, that he had a short time to accomplish his goals. He had a strong premonition that for him death would come somewhere on the civil rights trail.

"I cannot stop," he told me one day. "Not yet."

He said that another time when I went to him—on this occasion in St. Augustine, Florida—to check a rumor he had been killed. He survived a stabbing from another Negro in New York, and bore the scars of numerous attacks.

It was now 1968, and it had been almost thirteen years since King's career as a desegregation activist began.

Leader Dies Moments after Saying, "Precious Lord, take my hand."

In late March, against the advice of his associates and of government advisers, he announced that he would suspend other activities for a brief trip to Memphis, Tennessee, in support of striking black garbage workers.

The day before King left for Memphis, he said: "It really doesn't matter what happens now; I have been to the mountain top." A new national civil rights law had been passed, helped along with the demonstrations he led. Hotels, motels, and public eating facilities were at last open to all races. The "white only" signs were gone from drinking fountains, park benches, transportation facilities, and other public places. Unmolested, blacks were registering to vote in large numbers—and being elected to public office. King had won the Nobel Peace Prize for his work. He felt he had seen the fulfillment of his nonviolent goals.

He and his staff checked into the Lorraine Motel in Memphis late in the afternoon of April 1. In his first statement there, King said: "As I left Atlanta this morning, the pilot said over the public address system, 'We are sorry for the delay, but we have Dr. Martin Luther King on the plane and, to be sure that all bags were checked and that nothing would be wrong on the plane, we had to check on everything carefully. We have had the plane protected.'"

I had been on flights with King when some passengers would get off after he appeared on board, and ask for a different flight. They did not mind riding with him; they were afraid the plane would be blown up. In Memphis, he heard again of threats if he carried out plans to lead a garbage workers' march through the city. He ignored the threats.

"Like anybody else, I would like to live a long life," King told followers during an evening rally. "Longevity has its place, but I'm not concerned about that now. I just want to do God's will. He has allowed me to go up the mountain, and I've looked over, and I've seen the Promised Land. I may not get there with you, but I want you to know that we as a people will get to the Promised Land. So, I am happy tonight. I am not worried about anything. I'm not fearing any man. Mine eyes have seen the glory of the coming of the Lord."

Although violence had resulted already from one of the Memphis garbage workers' marches, King was planning another and bigger one. He would use the time until the march to develop a force of nonviolent marchers. That was his tactic everywhere. In a Mississippi church one night, King was schooling his crowd for nonviolence while associates on their hands and knees looked under pews for suspected dynamite. In the early days of his mission, he and other blacks attended nonviolence training sessions where they were spat upon, cursed, and slugged to strengthen their passive resistance to violence.

During the day of April 4, Federal District Judge Bailey Brown had a hearing concerning King's determination to conduct another march in the face of threats of violence. The Reverend Andrew Young, one of King's most trusted lieutenants, was asked by the jurist if the threats of violence would deter the civil rights leader.

"I would say that Dr. King would consider it a repudiation of his philosophy and his whole way of life," Young replied. Then he added, "I don't know when I have seen him as discouraged and depressed."

In the early evening of April 4, King and his staff made dinner plans to precede the night's rally. King walked out onto the motel's second floor balcony and stood chatting with two friends. One was the musician who would play that night. King asked him to play a spiritual, "Precious Lord, Take My Hand." It was to have been a time of celebration. Just two days before, President Johnson had signed the new Civil Rights Act that King had fought so hard to achieve.

As Dr. King stood on the balcony talking with his associates, a single rifle shot was fired. King fell to the floor mortally wounded. In an instant, the shot effectively brought to an end the civil rights movement of the 1960s. The police record said the fatal shot was fired from a cheap transient hotel at 422-1/2 Main Street, Room 5-B, which had been rented to a man registered as John Willard; and that the assassin escaped in a white Mustang automobile while King's crusaders were overcome by grief and anger.

Memphis was saved from a bloodbath that night because of a swiftly delivered federal court injunction against demonstrations, and the arrival of National Guardsmen to enforce the order. Memphis suffered one death and fifty injuries; other parts of the nation did not fare so well.

On Assassination Night, the skies of big cities in America were lit by the fires of passion and anguish. Blacks put the torch to large sections of Chicago, Washington, D.C., Philadelphia, and New York. The nation had not been so close to insurrection since the Civil War. Riots erupted in 125 cities in twenty-eight states, leaving forty-six dead, 2,600 injured, 21,270 arrested, and property damage estimated at forty-five million dollars.

An itinerant prison fugitive by the name of James Earl Ray became the prime suspect in the assassination, and he was indicted (in absentia) for murder on April 22. On June 8, as Attorney General Robert Kennedy, victim of another assassination, was being buried, Scotland Yard arrested Ray at a London airport. He had paid for a round-trip ticket to Europe with cash—still one of the mysteries in the case. He carried a gun, a Canadian passport, and an assumed name.

It was the Royal Canadian Mounted Police organization, sifting item by item through thousands of passports, which set the wheels in motion that led to Ray's arrest. He pleaded not guilty, but nine months later changed the plea to guilty.

Ray was sent to prison for ninety-nine years, but had he gone to trial he could have received the death penalty. He repudiated his guilty plea later, and asked for a new trial, charging that he had been pressured by ambitious lawyers into admitting the King murder. His request for a new trial was denied, and he was confined alone in a cell in a Tennessee prison, waiting for the year 2027 when he could be eligible for parole consideration. He died of liver failure in 1998 at the age of seventy.

On Sunday, April 7, I listened to a tormented sermon by Dr. Elam Davies at Chicago's 4th Presbyterian Church. He asked: "Why are we so blind to the lessons of history? Why are we so stupid as to think that we can get away with oppression or injustice, or plain indifference? We can't stop the march of events. We're not going to silence the cry of God's excluded ones . . .

"They've started to cry out already, haven't they? The land of the free and the home of the brave is an armed camp. Trucks full of federal troops ride down our beautiful Lakeshore Drive. I never thought I would see the day when police and soldiers with guns at the ready would be walking up and down outside my home. The sky is red with the frustrated fires of reverse racism and senseless hooliganism.

"You don't have to wait for America to be attacked by the enemies without. It will fall, unless we wake up, by the hand of enemies within. And these enemies within are not one color only . . . For some, it will take the refined way of doing nothing and caring less. For others, it will take the road of loot and shoot. There's no difference between them."

Dr. Martin Luther King, Jr., came home to Atlanta from Memphis in a jet airplane sent by President Johnson. Riding by his side was King's widow, Coretta, a woman of incredible spiritual strength in this hour of her grief. She directed most of the final arrangements for her husband and at her request his body lay in state in Sisters Chapel of Spelman College on the Atlanta University campus. For the next two days, thousands from Atlanta, from the nation beyond Atlanta, and from countries beyond this nation filed past the casket.

Ebenezer Baptist Church on Auburn Avenue in Atlanta is a modest red-brick structure. Its name came from the first book of Samuel in the Bible: "Then Samuel took a stone and set it between Mizpeh and Shen, and called the name of it Ebenezer, saying, hitherto hath the Lord helped us." Mourners came early to the church for the funeral on Tuesday, September 9; but even early was too late for most to find seats. The crowds overflowed onto the church grounds and into the city beyond. Assassination had brought peace for a spell to competing factions in the civil rights controversy.

When the eulogies were finished, the coffin was lifted onto the boards of a mule-drawn wagon, and the cortege moved slowly through the streets of Atlanta—up Auburn Avenue to Peachtree Street, out to Mitchell Street and to King's alma mater, Morehouse College. It was a route he had used many hundreds of times as he traveled from classrooms to his father's church where he would later become assistant pastor. Uncounted thousands followed the bier, silently, mournfully. The widow and her four young children—Bernice, Dexter, Martin Luther King III, and Yolanda—were next to the Reverend Ralph David Abernathy, loyal first assistant to King, who led the procession. Then came Vice President Hubert Humphrey; New York Governor Nelson Rockefeller; Mrs. John F. Kennedy, widow of the slain president; King's brother, the Rev. A. D. King; and Attorney General and Mrs. Robert Kennedy.

For three-and-a-half miles they walked the streets of Atlanta until they reached Morehouse and the memorial service arranged there. The murdered civil rights leader was then taken to Southview Cemetery to lie beside his grandfather—but only for a while. A magnificent Martin Luther King Center for Social Change was soon built with privately raised funds next door to Ebenezer, complete with library, classrooms for workshops, and auditorium. Outside in the courtyard a reflecting pool was built on several levels so there would always be movement of the waters. It was here on a platform in the center of the pool that Dr. King's remains eventually came.

The words on his burial monument, lit by an eternal flame, read: "Free at last! Free at last! Thank God Almighty, I'm free at last"—words penned by an obscure black preacher many years before the civil rights campaign of the mid-twentieth century.

Was this then the sunset of the civil rights movement in America? With Martin Luther King's going, was all that effort of the past twelve years canceled? It seemed so at this time of final tragedy in the young preacher's earthly sojourn. The power grabbers came swiftly after the funeral, as did accusations, bickering, finger-pointing.

In the last years of his life, Dr. King had been all too familiar with these problems among his following. Perhaps he dealt with them too softly, for he excused much wrong-doing. He often explained that "these are children" just learning the ways of polite society. "They don't know which side of the plate the fork goes on," he remarked one day to a critic. I recall the time one of his lieutenants was accused of stealing the Movement's money. King publicly forgave him and told how the man's family had been impoverished as the cost of his front-line duty with the crusade.

I remember when he turned publicly against the war in Vietnam before it was the popular thing to do—the charges of going communist, the hurt in his own people who sensed that their painful mission was being abandoned.

The day he took his stand on Vietnam, I interviewed him in a hotel room in Birmingham, Alabama. Pacing the floor in sock feet, he seemed to be in inner anguish, knowing that in a way he was indeed stepping ahead of the black movement in America and into world politics; and in another way he was turning against the individual who ordered the grand design of the Selma-to-Montgomery march: Lyndon Baines Johnson, president of the United States.

When Martin Luther King, Jr., left the scene there was sunset on one phase of the black movement, for it was never again the same; never again the same bold strokes, the outlandish ideas that turned into realities. But what follows every sunset is a new day, and that came, too. Some of those new days were stormy, and ever shall be; blustery, wet, and cold like Selma. And some of those new days brought the advent of new progress for blacks. By the thousands, they moved up the economic ladder, got out of poverty, got off welfare, held heads as high as anybody, voted, became a part of the American dream, ate where they chose, lived where they could afford it, earned a piece of the pie.

I recalled King's father, stalwart old "Daddy" King, sitting there at Spring Street School in Atlanta while his grandchildren were beginning their new school experience—the quiet confidence of the man in a new sunrise coming for them. Of all the victims of the civil rights movement, I felt most deeply for "Daddy" King, almost more than for young King's widow, Coretta, and the children. He remained a rock of faith through it all—the slaying of Martin, the drowning death of young A.D., Martin's brother, and finally in 1974 the unbelievable tragedy that befell his beloved life partner, Alberta.

Mrs. King, Sr., was shot to death by black gunman Marcus Wayne Chenault, 23, of Dayton, Ohio, in the presence of four hundred worshipers as Mrs. King played the organ in her husband's church. Worshippers subdued

Chenault, but not before he emptied two handguns, killing Mrs. King and Deacon Edward Boykin and wounding another worshiper, Mrs. Jimmy Mitchell. Chenault was convicted of first-degree murder and sentenced to be executed. He later was re-sentenced to life in prison and died after suffering a stroke in 1995.

In his son Martin's ascendancy in the racial movement, "Daddy" King received little public attention outside his church; but tough and firm he always was about his race, and that was a factor in his son's own strength. Once when Martin was a young boy, the two visited a shoe store and a clerk asked them to sit in a segregated section of the store. The senior King informed the clerk that they were there to buy shoes with the same kind of money every other customer used, and that they would be served where they sat or not at all. The store lost a customer that day, and this was years before an active movement to break segregation barriers in Atlanta.

More than a generation later, Coretta Scott King, widow of Dr. Martin Luther King, Jr., died in 2006. She was a powerful, though often silent, supporter of her husband. Paul Greenberg, editorial page editor for the *Arkansas Democrat-Gazette*, wrote in a column for the *Jewish World Review* that: "[She not only stood by] her husband but by her country . . . She bid us follow without needing to say a word. Did she ever give a memorable speech in her life? She didn't have to. All she had to do was appear, and the message was delivered. Queens are like that."

In this sunset of the huge crowds and many speeches surrounding civil rights, Coretta King's service beat them all, including the funeral of Dr. Martin Luther King, Jr., His was in the three-hundred-seat Ebenezer Baptist Church, where he and his father had preached, as uncounted crowds stood outside.

Coretta's was in the once small town of Lithonia in the New Birth Missionary Baptist Church, providing a huge seating capacity of ten thousand. Meanwhile, on presidential orders, flags flew at half staff in memory of the lady who kept the light of publicity always turned on her husband, not on herself.

President Bush and former Presidents Clinton, Carter, and the elder Bush all paid tribute to King's widow, along with speakers from Congress and others from the long years of the civil rights revolution. Lithonia itself provided a special feeling for these mourners, since in the long ago past it had allowed a haven for anti-black Ku Klux Klan members who were chased away from popular Stone Mountain several miles away. Mrs. King was buried beside her fallen husband at the King Memorial Center in Atlanta.

So ended the time on earth for the last of the "Big Three" of the civil rights era. The organization, however, remains in place to tell the story of America's "peaceful" revolution.

In the sunrise of a new day, I remember Andrew Young leading King's night marches in St. Augustine, Florida, calmly absorbing the punishment of segregationist attackers; then I remember Young as mayor of Atlanta, advising black people to "get smart" and stop complaining about their lot.

I see the evidence of blacks, clutching the freedom forced by the King campaign, rising to positions of respect and prominence in business and government—reflecting what they had achieved for the lives of oncoming generations of blacks.

I see once-embattled Southern communities where death and turmoil stalked the streets turn to the new sunrise and make peace with their black fellow citizens.

Would this new sunrise have occurred without King, without Birmingham, without Selma, without that "Dream" outpouring in Washington?

Al Kuettner looks through his files at his home in Gravette, Arkansas. Photo: Gravette News Herald

CHAPTER 17

2004–Looking Back Fifty Years Later

"I looked over Jordan and what did I see, comin' for to carry me home . . ."

—Negro spiritual

Was the Struggle Worth the Cost?

We have traveled many a mile in this story of two races, one black and one white, and it's time to pause, look back, and reflect on what we've seen and how far we've come. What did the "Civil Rights Revolution" in America accomplish? Was it worth the cost in struggle, pain, and lives? What remains to be done?

In 2004, on the fiftieth birthday of what was known as "the Movement," it was my strong conviction to seek answers to these questions by retracing my steps of a half-century earlier. At the age of ninety-one, I returned to Montgomery, to Birmingham, and to Selma. Of course, there had been many hot spots, but these three seemed to represent the whole picture of what it was all about.

As I began my trip I thought back over the history of the races in America. The ancestors of many of the white race came to these shores to escape the imperial policies of government in Europe and to make better lives in a new environment. The ancestors of many of the black race were dragged to these shores by money-hungry exploiters as slaves who were sold like real estate.

Like a sore that would not heal, the power of whites and helplessness of blacks festered and bubbled. Some lucky slaves would get away and find the Underground Railroad, a network of friendly whites who guided them to the "safe" North.

As time went on, the black race of forced immigrants spread out into mainly seventeen states and the District of Columbia. Slavery ended but they became the servant race.

As weeks, months, years, generations passed, the plight of African-Americans remained about the same—practically no education for most, no chance to vote, and no chance to make life any different. It was about the time two world wars ended that things began to be different. Returning troops included black soldiers who had seen a new world and dreamed of better futures. For a long time, talk was all it was because, in the South, white was white and superior, and black was black and inferior. But soon that wasn't good enough for guys who had crisscrossed the earth. They began to take advantage of educational institutions such as Tuskeegee Institute in Alabama and Atlanta University with its cluster of nearby colleges.

They and their children and grandchildren saw where the walls of intolerance stood. With their education, they saw their boundaries, one being running for public office. The aging soldiers could not see much for their own futures, but they could dream. Whites dominated elected offices. So the younger generations of their black brothers swung into step behind leaders like Dr. Martin Luther King, Jr. They cheered such long-sought events as the U.S. Supreme Court decision of 1954 and the Montgomery bus boycott of 1955. Black Americans had many ways of reaching for equality in those days. Their focus was on equal citizenship—for all. That became their national goal.

For example, in Atlanta, as most of the downtown white population drifted away to the suburbs, and the central city opened largely to black leadership, blacks used their voting rights to seek the previously unreachable: public office.

One of the young leaders was John Lewis, author of *Free at Last*, who while in his twenties organized voter registration drives and was an organizer and keynote speaker at the historic 1963 March on Washington. He later won election to the Atlanta City Council and then to Congress.

As I traveled, I thought of the turbulence of the Black Power movement and Roy Wilkins' words that: "The Negro has lost the ball in the high grass if he tries to go it without the cooperation of the 90 percent majority in this country." Wilkins was not in favor of King's massive crowd agitations, either; but Wilkins never explained why success had not been achieved with a less strenuous effort. King seemed to know, however, that nothing less would have succeeded.

I thought of the role played by the nation's political leadership— Presidents Kennedy and Johnson. I regularly had been bombarded for verification that the president had any connection with the civil rights revolution. Who was it in the war room of the White House—watching in disbelief at the panic at Ole Miss? Who gave the order to call out the troops? And what about President Kennedy's brother, Robert, who as presidential adviser, attorney general, and senator traveled the land to bring civil rights reasoning out of madness? Yes, that was the senator jumping off a platform at the University of Alabama football stadium and into a mass of angry students. That was Bobby, walking the walk, seeking reason in this bitter battle for racial equality.

As I reached Montgomery, perhaps it was sentimental to first visit the spot where I had met a young African-American named Martin Luther King, Jr. It was in the middle 1950s and racial trouble was brewing. There was a look of concern and fear on most faces: Who is this white guy in their church?

There was a hint of suspicion that day at the Dexter Avenue Baptist Church (now renamed the Dexter Avenue King Memorial Baptist Church) in Montgomery, across the drive from the state capitol. An usher asked my name, someone in church engaged me in conversation. "Oh, you are a reporter? Who do you work for?"

On my visit in 2004, however, none of that suspicion was visible. The style that I noticed most was celebration. It was in their faces, it was in their church sermon, and especially it was in their singing. "Amen" became a cheer lasting ten minutes by my watch; five hundred voices backed up by piano, organ, and marching instruments fueled a spirit that lingered all through the after-church fellowship. There was nothing artificial about it; this was real and it was impressive.

Many with whom I spoke after church were reluctant to talk or think about the past; the focus was "now." Everyone wanted to talk with this reporter. "Issues that are dividing us are being healed," a church member said proudly.

Well-dressed young people mixed easily with their elders, a minority who had lived through the whole adventure. I would guess that most were the children, grandchildren, and perhaps even the great-grandchildren of their African-American relatives who had been through the struggle. They chattered away like most young folks: "Did you pass math?" "What college did you pick?"

When I managed a farewell from those around me, the next stop was the steel city of the South, Birmingham, and its beautiful downtown park. It was from this park that television screens worldwide featured some of the worst demonstrations of the racial crusade. Young blacks, in this case, were pushing their effort to have free use of downtown eateries and public restrooms at the same time that Congress heatedly was debating legislation that would answer the question.

Birmingham had been my first real assignment, and what an assignment it turned out to be. Birmingham meant coal and iron being taken from the ground, at spots very deep into the earth. It was steel, burned from the iron, turned into plate for America's fighting Navy in World War II. It was tough, hard work, work that forged opinions as hard as the finished steel from the plants. That's the kind of town Birmingham was proud to be.

Birmingham is not a bad town; it's a great town in many ways. I still believe that Birmingham would have found compromise on the race issue without all the dogs and fire hoses. Politics and feisty elements got into it, and like someone said, "It just busted the dam." But think about what ultimately happened. A selection of seventy white men from all walks of life, and a strong element of black leaders, went into a large room at the Chamber of Commerce and stayed there wrestling with the problem until respect for each other emerged first and solutions emerged next.

Now, it was forty years later and my memory was still forged like a slab of iron into the heart of this place. In the year 2004 I could not avoid thinking of those days of racial turmoil back in the 1960s. I wondered: Was all the fighting worth it? The dogs and fire hoses? The tragedy of little children bombed to death in the Sixteenth Street Baptist Church?

I could not forget a small, dark-skinned boy who, on a morning of demonstrations, walked down the steps of the Sixteenth Street Baptist Church. I'll never forget how he looked straight ahead, squaring his skinny shoulders as if to shake off fear; how he walked to a sidewalk that bordered the park. He knew that the end of this little experience would be jail for his demonstrating.

As he passed me, reciting over and over the word "freedom," I asked him what he meant and he replied he didn't know. Fifty yards down the walkway he lost his freedom temporarily as he was taken into a fenced jailhouse yard. In my sharp memories of that day in the South, I thought of that boy. Did he finish school and get a job? Does he remember that day in his hometown when he went to jail? Does he think his long-ago actions made a difference in his life, or in the lives of his friends?

It was Sunday afternoon. Visitors strolled on new walks in the park. There was peace and quiet. The memories seemed from a time very long ago. A young black man crossed my path and we paused to talk. When I asked him if he thought all the racial trouble was necessary, he promptly replied, "Certainly," as though everyone knew that. But as we talked, his attention was aroused by a small group of black young people, about high school age. They were having fun mimicking one of the demonstrations. "They think they are winning but they are losing all the time," he said.

I said good-bye for I was eager to get to Selma, fifty miles west of Montgomery. Why would I want to go to Selma when it had brought up such bad memories of my assignment there forty years earlier? Surely with all the bitterness this poor town had endured then, the feelings could not have healed yet. How wrong could I get!

When I crossed the Pettus Bridge and entered downtown Selma that day in 2004, I soon found that the desegregation process, as I had heard and disbelieved, had been settled. From all I discovered in the next several days, the memories of Selma's past were remembered mostly in local museums. The real world for that once-sad town was quite different.

Selma is an old town with an international atmosphere. In the early 1800s it was occupied by European merchants who had come to the states to buy the cotton that grew in the region. They stayed for business and left their mark. One of the businesses was to be my hotel, an exquisite example of European architecture built in 1837. It had been faithfully preserved on Water Avenue beside the Alabama River. It's called the St. James.

"We have put you in a room on the second floor," the clerk explained. "'That way you will be in a room off the river view. Just open your door to the deck and enjoy."

I did just that, and what a treat. The Alabama River is wide at the hotel deck. Someone in a fast-moving boat sped past. The arch of the Pettus Bridge provided a special scene up high to my right. The river once brought royalty and business barons to the hotel dock. Such travelers brought big economic gifts as well as ideas and philosophies.

It was a thoughtful time, and the thoughts flowed like that river. I thought of how the 1954 Supreme Court decision that struck down segregation in public schools began to level the playing field for black children throughout the South and across the country—and how education is fundamental to so much else in life. I reflected on the fact that one black child born into a middle-class family in Birmingham in 1954, Condoleezza Rice, had grown up to become secretary of state.

In a November 2005 interview with *Ebony* magazine Dr. Rice reflected on the importance of education in achieving success. She said her personal heroine is Dr. Dorothy Height, a major leader of the civil rights movement in the 1960s and president of the National Council of Negro Women for more than forty years. "People who had the foresight to see, as the struggle unfolded, that education was the key to having a whole generation of people who were ready to take advantage once the United States came to terms with segregation were my heroes," Dr. Rice said.

I thought of how the Selma to Montgomery march, which galvanized the entire civil rights effort, was engineered in a think session of black youths in which a few boys called out, "Let's walk to Montgomery and see the governor." (The march worked, seeing the governor did not.) The King movement had been established to focus on voting rights, use of public facilities such as water fountains, and freedom in public places such as theaters and restaurants. It had confronted the never-never attitude that stopped the first march at the Pettus Bridge—the same attitude that had wrought havoc in Mississippi and else-where in the South, bringing out the armed forces.

Had Selma really changed? Because I had been trained to first be dubious, I was skeptical as I drove around the city. I drove past the voter registration building. A few men, white and black, were entering the building. During the bitter voter uprising a man trying to force his way in would have encoun-tered a husky sheriff's deputy (white) and been beaten to the floor or dragged to a vehicle and to jail. A black youth noticed my unfamiliar car and threw up an arm in a welcoming gesture. I slowed down and we gave each other a distant high five and a horn toot.

I realized towns like Selma, Birmingham, Montgomery, and many others have begun to outlive the shadows of race reaction. There has developed, to say the least, acceptance of federal determination to protect the ability of cit-izens and their families to receive equalized education unhampered by restric-tive racial rules, to attend public events based on ability to pay a ticket price, and to live in peace "from sea to shining sea." New generations will have to deal with the myriad other social problems that always have concerned citi-zens on the way up.

Before leaving Selma, I went for one last visit to the overlook deck outside my bedroom. It was that early part of a Southern morning when it looks like God sort of mixed up all his colors for the dawn. A fish jumped in the river, and I settled down in my chair. I thought how I had asked many passersby on this long trail, "Was it worth it?" All who answered said yes, it had to be done, there was no other way. One man commented, somewhat sadly, I thought, "It all had to go to the bitter end. This was a war of ideas." He was right, it was a collision of ideas—a collision that still has not completely come to rest.

I thought of George Corley Wallace, the governor of Alabama at the height of the civil rights struggle. Wallace, who died in 1998, publicly apol-ogized for his role in the civil rights revolution. "I am sorry," he said.

Guess I got to dreaming because I remembered way back in Georgia where a white teacher settled a racial problem when she got a little white boy to touch a little black boy's kinky hair for the first time; and I recalled that sad old Negro preacher, standing in the hot remains of his burned church. I thought about Martin Luther King, Jr., and his own dream speech, his stand for racial justice, and a Southern governor's efforts to keep the races separate.

I thought of the legacy left by those white and black who in spite of the bigots were determined that the races could live together in a country where men and women accepted and respected those of all colors who crossed their paths in peace.

As I relaxed in my chair on the deck above the river, in this serene setting that once was in chaos, I thought of all those civil rights conflicts of another generation—and how Americans will deal with the conflicts in the future. My thoughts were joined by a song that I must have heard in one of the churches along this trail: *"I looked over Jordan and what did I see . . ."*

Chapter 1

Page 2: *Essays in the History of the American Negro* (New York Publishers, 1945) pp. 203-204.

Page 6: Southern members of the American Society of Newspaper Editors, wisely realizing that the story of the transition in education resulting from the court decisions of the 1950s and 1960s would be of lasting importance, conceived the idea of a strictly objective report on developments. The Southern Education Reporting Service was formed on May 11, 1954, with Virginius Dabney, editor of the Richmond, Va., *Times Dispatch* as chairman; Thomas R. Waring, editor of the *Charleston News and Courier* as vice chairman; and, by action of the board of directors on June 6, C.A. "Pete" McKnight, editor of the Charlotte, N.C., *News*, as executive director. The Fund for the Advancement of Education provided the first funding. The information arm of the organization was a factual monthly publication, *Southern School News*. The Reporting Service and *Southern School News* never took sides; their sole objective was the search for facts in the complex issue of school desegregation. During its ten-year existence, the Reporting Service was directed by the leading newspaper editors of the South. Upon completion of its mission, the vast amount of accumulated documents, reports, charts, and figures were placed in the library of Fisk University in Nashville, Tenn., for use by researchers, writers and scholars.

Page 7, 8, 13, 14: Quotations on the oral arguments in *Brown v. Board of Education* are from *Landmark Briefs and Arguments of the Supreme Court of the United States: Constitutional Law, Vols. 49 and 49A*, University Publications of America Inc.

Chapter 5

Page 50: Judge Seybourne Lynne's quotes are from the *New York Times*, June 7, 1963.

Page 52: The statements of Nicholas deB. Katzenbach and President John F. Kennedy are from the *New York Times*, June 12, 1963.

Chapter 9

Page 103: The statements of Ralph Bunche, James Farmer, and John Lewis are from the *New York Times*, August 28, 1963.

Page 128: Kuettner notes: The seats Merriman Smith and I had were on concrete steps of the Lincoln Memorial. We were never more than 50 to 100 feet from the speakers' stand.

Page 129: Kuettner notes: As King began speaking, I moved closer to his stand; Smith had the prepared speech early and he gave the go-ahead to the Washington bureau the instant that King spoke. When King hit the dream part, Smith shifted gears. Each of us began taking down the new text as King spoke. This also was a dangerous moment. Washington detectives and police swept the scene, but all was quiet in that huge crowd.

Page 140: Kuettner notes: Sheriff Davis had only 100 deputies to guard King and others, but there was no trouble.

Page 141: Kuettner notes: I was covering at the motor lodge when King tried and failed to get registered for a room.

Chapter 16

Prior to Dr. Martin Luther King's death in 1968, the author of this book left the ranks of UPI to take another position, leaving it up to an experienced and dedicated staff to carry on the work of covering the movement. The reports in this chapter are largely from that work, as well as the author's reprise of King's life written for UPI in April 1968.

Index